# Funny Side Up

Tommy:
You is a Gooda Kids!
I'd like you as a son...
but I alread have five!

Remember to Always keep a "uniform" life... and you will never go Bare Butt...

Your friend in Short Pants...

8/16

# *Funny Side Up*®

*Al D. Squitieri*

**Writers Club Press**
San Jose   New York   Lincoln   Shanghai

Funny Side Up®

All Rights Reserved © 2000 by Al D. Squitieri, Sr.

No part of this book may be reproduced or transmitted in any form or by any means, graphic, electronic, or mechanical, including photocopying, recording, taping, or by any information storage retrieval system, without the permission in writing from the publisher.

Writers Club Press
an imprint of iUniverse.com, Inc.

For information address:
iUniverse.com, Inc.
5220 S 16th, Ste. 200
Lincoln, NE 68512
www.iuniverse.com

ISBN: 0-595-09551-8

Printed in the United States of America

To my beautiful children:
Theresa
    Anthony
        Joseph
            Lorraine
                Arlene
                    Al, Jr.
                        Christopher
                          Danielle
                            David
                              Vicki…

and to my wife Anne, whose patience makes our house a home…

# Contents

Introduction
Que Sara' Sara' ...................................................................ix

The Last Time I Had a Baby
or The Alpha and Omega ......................................................1

"Give us this day our daily bread..." ........................................5

The Case of the Missing Yoohoo ............................................9

Moses Merely Parted the Sea ................................................13

Never A Dull Morning .........................................................17

Smoke Gets in My Eyes .......................................................19

Dohickies, Dingamabobs and Whatchamacallits ....................21

"No Cost, Just Aggravation" .................................................25

A Stitch in Time ..................................................................29

Freebies in Burgerland .........................................................33

K-9 Section Eight ................................................................37

Blooming Blunder Awards ...................................................41

I Goof...You Blunder ..........................................................49

"Them" is a Fighting Word ..................................................53

Embarrassing Moments .......................................................57

A Flight in Shivering Armor ................................................59

I Get Letters...Lots of Letters ..............................................61

I Also Write Letters... .........................................................65

Absence Makes the Heartburn Stronger ............................................. 69
Good Ol' Southern Hostility ............................................................ 73
Men on Mall Benches ..................................................................... 77
"Picky, Picky, Picky" ....................................................................... 81
"Restaurants Everywhere…But No Place to Eat" ............................ 85
An Offer You Can't Refuse ............................................................. 89
Someday Was Yesterday ................................................................. 93
…And then There Were None ...................................................... 101

# Introduction
# Que Sara' Sara'

I was born and raised on the Upper Eastside of New York City, one month and three blocks apart from my wife to be. Shakespeare would call it *"Kismet:* "a divinity that shapes our ends…" I agree, it was predestination on God's part.

Her name is Anna, as was my mother's, and was the only thing we had in common. Her mother was Irish, her father Italian. Myself a full blooded Neapolitan. She worked from the age of 16. I was a typical *"Wise Guy"*, who shot pool with the local *"Don"* and did whatever was needed to get the "bread" for Broadway shows, movies and restaurants. There were lots of girls to share weekends with, but things change, and when you least expect it.

To keep myself legal and my parents off my back, I took occasional employment: I did time at *McGraw-Hill Publishing* with a sister, a year at the post office with a brother-in-law; and time as a plumber's helper with a friend. Having a steady job was a rare thing for me. I believed working for a living was for those robot like "suits" whose whole lives were their jobs. Sardine rides on the subway, 7 a.m. calls and once per-week pay checks were a major influence on that kind of thinking.

Anna, who changed her name to a younger sounding Anne, was working at the *New York Telephone Company,* and I was doing a stint at the *Children's Aid Society of New York.*

This brief employment was part of God's Plan. Anne's girlfriend "Lou Lou" told her about a guy she worked with at the Society, whom she wanted Anne to meet. Anne said no, I have this guy I want *you* to meet. While they discussed the matter of "my guy" or "your guy", they both said in unison: *"Here he comes now!"* I turned out to be the same guy! From then on, she chased me—until I caught her.

We married and our first apartment was a two room, cold water flat on Second Avenue. The toilet was in a broom closet without elbowroom, forcing one to back-in. Often times we heard guests banging their heads trying to retrieve their draws. The clawed-foot bathtub in the kitchen was hidden under an enameled steel cover, which substituted for a countertop. Our bathroom sink, A.K.A the kitchen sink, did double duty. But it was ours—and larger than the single bedroom we shared at Anne's parents.

We were a happy twosome. Time was our own. Food servings were not yet rationed—and consisted of large, thick steaks. Donuts by the dozen, Hostess Devil Dogs by the box, and milk by the carton. I actually ate whole Twinkies rather than licking leftover wrappers.

We had breakfast in bed, snacks by the TV, and coffee on the stoop. Meals were peaceful candlelight dinners. It wasn't necessary to gulp meals to keep one's share. Our love life, like our food supply, was plentiful and uninterrupted.

Then the rabbit died…ten times. Theresa was the first of ten. She interrupted our days and nights changing our very lives. No longer just a happy couple, we were now a proud family of three. It's been so long since my wife Anne and I setout to multiply the earth, I can barely remember back to B.C.—Before Children! Like the frog in the pot of boiling water, you really don't know what you're getting into until it's too late. To avoid further brain drain, I leave kid's birth dates and names up to Anne. Until I get them straight, *"Hey you"* will have to suffice. With the added thirteen grandkids, I need a roster to keep track. Add a few daughters-in-law, sons-in-law, *their* in-laws; pets, peeves and peccadilloes, it becomes overwhelming.

While Married 44 years, we have survived the raising of ten kids, which makes raising the Titanic a piece-of-cake. Reflecting upon the difference between B.C., D.C and A.C. (During and After the little darlings) the contrast is remarkable. I don't mean *"those good ol' days"*—since it has been getting *"gooder"* all the time, but those changes between Anne, myself and life in general. Call it reminiscence or nostalgia, the result is the same: momentous events worth recalling.

My diary was a newspaper column entitled: *FUNNY SIDE UP*, which I wrote for a dozen small weeklies. Readers believed it was written for their enjoyment, when in reality, they were my weekly sessions on "The Couch". I think of it as my years spent in James Thurber's quandary. In retrospect I'm amazed I've kept it together thus far, although Anne doubts the validity of that statement. I say it was due to my being catatonic for forty years, but she says the only thing I was "out-of" was the house.

The following stories are from that weekly diary, which allow insight into the mind of a man surrounded by ten children, assorted dogs, cats and goldfish. They also invoke sympathy from my readers—not for me, but for Anne. It seems they see her as an Anne of Ark, and me as the consuming fire. Judge for yourself, dear reader, and tell me: what did I do wrong?

## The Last Time I Had a Baby
### or
## The Alpha and Omega

Having a baby is considered a natural occurrence. That depends on who is having the baby. From the first, till the last, it was the same torturous experience for me. I have this problem when near someone who is delivering: I throw-up. I could never overcome that feeling of panic when the mother-to-be says: *"I think I'm ready!"*

My first lesson in Obstetrics 101 came in New York City. It was after midnight during one of that city's worst snowstorm. A police car noticed me standing coatless and shoeless in the snow. I was trying to hail a cab, a bus, a stolen car…

After I told the cops I was having a baby, (quickly correcting myself) they asked where was the mother-to-be? I had left her upstairs in my rush to the hospital.

Anne rode between two of New York's Finest, while I sat on riot guns, gas masks, stale donuts and empty coffee cups. *"Please lady…"* begged one officer, *"...have it now, we need a new squad car!"* *"Oh...I think I'm going to throw-up!"* I said. *"That won't get us a new unit!"* said the other cop.

The first was Theresa. With Vicki the Last, I promised this one would be different. When Anne said those words: *"I think I'm ready!"* I sprang into action.

*"O.K., stay calm everyone..."* I said, *"don't panic, I'll take care of everything!"* Crossing the dinning room, I hit the water Anne had dropped when the bubble burst. Sliding on the seat of my wet underwear, I headed for the phone...feet first.

*"I knew it!"* cried Anne, *"I knew it, he's doing it again.* "God help me, he's doing it again!"

I was determined to be in complete control. I was not. While Anne called the doctor and hospital, I was shaking in my shorts, pushing my arms through 3/4 sleeves of a size 14 bright red coat. Anne was super calm, while I was cirri-comic shaggy dog: dripping underwear, torn coat sleeves up to my elbows, and a seriously upset stomach.

In the past, "Speedy" had dropped the bundle in twenty minutes from go. Trouble was I never knew when go started. She would countdown without me knowing, assuring me the pains were only three minutes apart. Why she had to torture me I can't figure. Why not go when they are five minutes apart? Is she playing chicken with the stork or what?

I turned the car around and kept the engine running, saving one whole minute. With the passenger door open, suitcase loaded, we were off! We were making good time: me the suitcase and...oops! *"I knew it!"* I insisted, *"I was only practicing!"* With her arms folded over her ever-falling belly, she snapped at me: *"Sure you were. Open the door!"*

We were a few blocks from the hospital on a dark side street when: Thump! Thump! Thump! A flat. Anne said this would never make a movie. No one would believe it. I started changing the flat in the dark.

No, I did not have a flashlight. Why would I? Nothing else had been planned. Suddenly from out of the darkness I heard a thundering noise. A horse resembling a German Shepherd was galloping toward me—barking like a dog. In two shakes of his tail, I was in the car. Anne was having belly laughs at my expense, ignoring her pain. He would allow me one lug nut, then come charging again, sending me back in the car.

Finally at the hospital, I leaned on the night bell for what seemed like an hour. Most likely the night nurse was making rounds, collecting all that forbidden candy from sleeping patients. Then she appeared—Big Bertha. She opened the door and said: *"Oh, it's 'you' again!"* I said, *"I have an emergency!"* *"Again...?"* she said, *"you have one every year!"*

The reception nurse was just out of candy strips, and still friendly. Convinced her nursing certificate from a trade school made her an equal to any Obstetrician; she tried to calm me. She started taking information like we were renting a motel room. *"Miss..."* I said with forced calmness, *"...if you don't hurry, you're going to have a mess on your carpet!"*

*"Relax sir. This must be your first!"* I told her it was my tenth, and she was in big trouble. *"OOhhhh!"* said Anne. *"Hurry Miss!"* Suddenly, this seasoned pro was running in circles, pushing buttons and shouting: *"Oh Miss Bertha, come quickly!"*

It was girl number five. That evened the score: five boys and five girls. Her doctor thought Anne was fertile enough to break the *Guinness Book of World Records,* which at the time was a mere 69. With alterations, it was the Omega.

What makes a man worry? Its because she is the mother of my children and the wife of my youth. The woman I loved for the best part of my life—in every way.

## "...Give us this day our daily bread, and make it two loaves please!"

Make it two loaves please, was my daily prayer.

No matter what you might have heard to the contrary, believe this: It's exactly 10 times as costly to raise ten kids as it is to raise one. Everything is larger, therefore more expensive.

The two-room apartment became a seven-room house. The hidden bathtub had increased to two full, inefficient baths. The two-seat sport coupe became a 10-passenger station wagon, and the grocery bill rocketed to atmospheric heights. We went from the calm of Shangri-La, to the chaos of Dulles International. Someone was always leaving or arriving. There was pushing, shoving, waiting in lines for meals, phone and bathroom reservations. Missing was the traffic controller, who would have suffered mental exhaustion on his first shift.

Easy on the milk meant the gallon must last the night. Toothpaste, shampoo, cereal and hot dogs came in "Family Size", and the utility bills were electrifying. I hated praying for "Extra Large" this and "Jumbo Size" that, but food moved very fast around here. It was like eating soup with a fork: it just got away from me. They ate everything that wasn't moving so I thought about selling the dining room chairs and serving buffet, since meals didn't last long enough to sit down. But I was afraid someone would run into me with a fork, that utensil they used as a weapon

This on-going battle of survival drove me to my knees many times. A prayer I remember vividly was a plea to the Lord akin to that of Joshua, before my walls came tumbling down. While I had His attention, I thought I'd speak with Him—man to Deity, with all due respect. I humbly pleaded, Lord I'm sure You know what it's like having a large family, which I'm sure You are proud of, but I must confess, I'm not exactly bubbling over at this moment, in fact, I'm depressed.

What should I say when people ask me what's it like having ten children? Should I say it's heavenly? Granted, there have been some bright spots (I can't recall any right now) but having ten kids is like dental flossing with piano wire: it keeps me on edge. You say in the 127th Psalm: *"Lo, children are a heritage of the Lord...as arrows, so are children. Happy is the man that hath his quiver full of them."* True my quiver is full, and I have my fill of them, but Lord, it is hard to be grateful when we have given up so much of ourselves for our children: Things like steak, sanity and solitude. Broadway shows have been replaced by television. Dinner at Sardi's is now a coupon at Arby's. A night out is an ice cream cone at a mall. Like Rodney Dangerfield, I too get no respect...or dessert.

When I left the house this A.M., Anne was making three dozen homemade donuts. When I came home for lunch, they were gone. I craved those donuts all morning. Three dozen for crying out loud! Where's mine? Where's mine!

Sorry! Excuse me Lord. It irritates me. Like the case of the missing Fudgie. Anne bought a dozen Fudgies. That's one each. I didn't feel like a Fudgie just then, so I put mine in the freezer. Later that night I felt like a Fudgie.

*"Who ate my Fudgie?"* I asked. *"Why are you shouting at this hour?"* asked Anne. *"Because I want my Fudgie! Who ate my Fudgie?"*

*"Oh, was that your Fudgie Dad?"* asked a voice from the security of darkness. *"I thought you didn't want it!" "Spinach Pie I don't want! Fudgies I want!"* I said.

*"Look at you…"* Anne said, *"You are losing control!"* I wasn't getting it, and neither was she. Yes Lord, I did lose control, but I was ready for a Fudgie, and ate corn flakes instead…and with skimmed milk for crying out loud. When Anne's on a diet, everyone's on a diet. What's that Lord? Yes, true, You do put-up with me provide even when I'm not worthy. Right, You do forgive and forget when I screw-up. I know, I should be the father that You are to me: show tolerance, patience, and unconditional love, since I didn't merit Your Love. This is all true, Lord, but enough already with the kids!

Well, I'm glad I got that off *YOUR* chest. I feel much better now. It always helps to talk father to Father. *Shalom!*

## The Case of the Missing Yoohoo

I don't recall ever telling my kids about my young life of hardships. I don't remember having any. If we were poor, my parents did a good job of hiding it from us. The worse hardship I could think of was walking six New York City blocks to school, flapping the soul of my shoe back into place each time it folded under foot. That always brought a visit to the Third Avenue shoe store, begging for "P.F.Flyers" instead of leather shoes.

I had it made from the start. I never had to fight for my share since I always had more than I could swallow. My parents owned a Mom and Pop candy store on the Upper East Side. Being the luckiest kid on the block, I had a soda fountain at my fingertips. I could make anything my grubby heart desired, but my choice was *"egg creams"* by the gallon. The poundage of candy was nothing more than snacks after the chocolate malts.

On our rush out the door, my siblings and I would detour behind the candy counter to snatch the profits. We dipped into the jars of *Baby Ruth, Clark Bar, Mary Jane, Mallo Cup*, and the ever popular, *Good and Plenty*. Pop would say: *"God Bless!"* making the sign of the cross. As we grew up, our looting increased to money and cigarettes, while Pop's chant always intrigued us. We finally asked mother to explain. She said he was blessing us as we dipped into the goodies. It reminded him of going to church: when entering and leaving, one always dipped their fingers into the Holy Water at the door: *"God Bless"* he repeated reverently. With that much blessing, his kids should have become two priests and three nuns.

In our neighborhood we had siren that went off every day at exactly 12 Noon. To the kids, it meant movie house prices were going up from .12 cents to a whopping .20 cents. To the other kids the increase meant the loss of candy money, but I got there with my pockets full of goodies, thanks to Pop.

I had a best friend, Peewee. Being inseparable, we were teased with names like: "bookends" and "Ditto and Ditto", because you never saw one without the other. This particular Saturday, this adventurous twosome was broke and the twelve cents needed for the movies seemed like an impossible sum of cash. It was nearing deadline, and we had no idea were to get the money. We sat reading the small four page *"Coming Attractions"* pamphlets they gave out on our last week's visit.

We sat in my father's storeroom racking our brains, while sitting among dozens of cases of soda. There was: *Coke, Pepsi, Canada Dry, Dr.Pepper, 7 Up,* and a chocolate drink called *"Yoohoo"* which Yogi Berra claimed he loved as much as baseball. Peewee made the comment about all the bottles being full, and could we even imagine drinking them all. We both looked around at the bottles, full of soda, but there were no empty bottles. Peewee asked where did my father keep the empties? Suddenly, we both had eyes as big as hubcaps. In unison, we both let out a scream: "**DEPOSIT!**"

The empties were in another area, right under my father's nose. He kept them where he could see them so the *"Soda Guy"* wouldn't cheat him on his count. How do we get deposit money on full bottles? There was one solution: we had to empty them. The deposit was two cents per bottle. We needed six bottles a piece to get the needed twelve cents. *"Well, lets get started…"* Peewee said, *"we don't have much time!"* "To do what?" I asked. *"Drink 'em"* he said.

Yoohoo is a sweet, thick chocolate drink that could satisfy with one bottle. Perhaps, with a serious craving, you might down two bottles. But six bottles is beyond tolerance.

With our stomachs bloated, and taste buds overwhelmed, we still had an added problem: where do we deposit my father's empty bottles? My Dad was not a CPA, but he could figure twelve bottles coming—when none were going, didn't add up. So, it was down the street to *"Jimmy's Candy Store"* which was on our way to the movies four blocks away. I naturally had to wait outside, being the kid from *"Tony's Candy Store"* up the street.

We had less than ten minutes to make the four block run to the *"Cosmo Theater"* before the noon whistle. We started at a pace that could have brought us a Gold Metal in track. Being loaded down with Yoohoo took its toll. After two blocks, we were down to a Silver Metal. By the last block, the Bronze was out.

Reaching the ticket booth, we were pale green in color and gasping for breath. The six bottles of Yoohoo had churned into milk shakes in our bellies. As we pushed our ticket money through the half-moon slot, the noon whistle blew. The cashier, staring in wonderment, said: *"You guys just made it…I think!"* While the triple feature and 25 cartoons rolled-on, Peewee and I had side-by-side toilet stalls, heaving up our guts. What a waste of movies, money and Yoohoo.

What is the moral of this story? Never drink more than you can handle? Never run four blocks on a full stomach? Never steal your father's inventory? Perhaps all of the above. But the strange thing is, I probably could have asked my Dad for the money, which meant conning him for Peewee's share. Worse yet, the innocent victim of this scheme was the poor Soda Guy who was accused of "stiffing" my father for twelve empties.

But it was Peewee's ideas that got us in trouble, although he says it was vice versa. Like the time we got caught smoking in his mother's bathroom. In haste to throw the lit cigarettes in the toilet, *SOMEONE'S* cigarette landed in a window curtain. The material, a matching set to the shower curtain, was made of lightweight plastic, which instantly started smoldering with dense, toxic smoke…but, that's another story…

## Moses Merely Parted the Sea

Getting ten children to church on time is a feat comparable to those of Samson or Moses, but than Samson merely brought down the house, my kids can do that before breakfast. And Moses, he moved a few thousand people with the help of Pillars of Clouds and Fire. All I had was the Hand of Anne, and a '69 Chevy, with a leaky radiator.

Just imagine taking a number to get into the bathroom. It takes special skills to live in a house with seven rooms, 1 1/2 baths, a wife, 10 kids, a pony resembling a German Shepherd, and a cat who drinks from a fishbowl containing two neurotic goldfish named: *"Dinner"* and *"Dessert"*.

If eight children is enough, than ten is more than enough. Meals resemble feeding time at the zoo. My two-legged piranhas clean a 20-pound turkey still in flight. How do we do it? It's a matter of timing—which I lack. I'm always too late because I'm too slow. I have fork marks on the back of both hands, get to lick the Twinkie wrappers, and always the last to get a number for the bathroom.

Sunday mornings are life threatening. One can get trampled to death in the charge for the bathroom. I have tried every trick to get my fair share of bathroom rights. I've pounded on the door shouting, *"It's the plumber!"* *"Yea, right Dad, nice try!"* I've tried threatening them with my authority:

*"In this house I'm number one at all times!" "Not in here you're not!"* Anne's voice shot back.

Finally, after 11 showers/baths, and 40 gallons of hot water, I got a glimpse of Bunk Hill. Strewn across the battlefield were: 18 towels, 10 face clothes, 4 face towels, an assortment of socks and underwear, and my bath robe used for a floor mat. The last of the soap was a tiny piece sitting at the tub drain. After emptying the tub of: two empty shampoo bottles, one airplane, one truck, three boats, a soggy comics section of the Sunday paper, and one familiar sock, it was my turn.

Wiping the steamed mirror, I watched myself bleeding to death shaving with a community razor. My wife claimed that was called *"bleeding out bad blood!"* She brought that up now, because an hour earlier I had yelled at the kids for making streamers of my typewriter ribbon. Between swinging of the medicine cabinet mirror, opening and closing of the vanity doors, I managed to get three razor nicks and two black and blue knee caps. Looking down at the vanity, I found the toothpaste tube twisted beyond hope. The sink, with tri-color swirls looked like a birthday cake decorated by Foster Brooks.

I was ready for my cold shower, which fittingly, is given to mental patients. I placed one foot in the tub: *"Hurry Dad, we'll be late for church!"* Beep! Beep! Sticking bits of toilet paper to my face, I dressed running to the car. We were only three miles from the church, being on time should be easy right? Landing troops on a beachhead is easy, we're talking difficult. We landed at 11:10, in time to form a colorful parade. The usher insisted upon herding 12 people down the main drag to the front row. I assumed punishment for being tardy. I could almost hear an announcer at a fashion show: *"Here we have Mrs. Squitieri wearing last years coat. Notice the gracefulness of the hanging hem. And here is Mr. Squitieri…wearing one shoe!"*

The cattle hustler is pulling at my coat sleeve, trying to drag us down front to a waiting audience. As I pleaded with him to allow us to crawl under the back pew, he said: *"I'm sorry sir, I have my orders from upstairs!"* Does God make seating arrangements too?

The commotion woke those already asleep. They were confused: was it an Exodus or an invasion? With the Squitieris it could be either. It appeared the usher was winning the tug-of-war, until Anna The Hun took charge. She gave him a look that would have stopped the Egyptian army in pursuit of Moses and Company. But then, Moses only had a rod, Anne had *"The Look"*. The shaken usher retreated. Then, as of old, Eve ignored the warnings of the forbidden pew, removed the rope and entered into the unpardonable sin in the eyes of the usher. Then I, as Adam of old, followed her into decadence, followed by my wayward kids. The pastor's opening remarks boomed out over the P.A.: *"I was glad when they said unto me, 'let us go into the house of the Lord…BUT…let us be on time!"* Every eye in the place turned to the 12 red-faced latecomers trying to crawl out of sight. I replied: *"Amen brother!"* …with toilet paper stuck to my cheek.

## Never A Dull Morning

Dark, rainy mornings are perfect for sleeping, unless you have ten kids at home. In that case the privilege of sleeping soundly past 6 a.m. is not one of your luxuries. The daily cacophonous symphony consists of slamming doors, opening and closing the refrigerator, thumping the steam iron, and the clatter of multiple butter knives hitting the stainless steel kitchen sink. The rousing finale comes with the slamming of the front door on their way out to school or work…one at a time. Heaven forbid, they all leave together.

The night before, I read them the riot act about early morning considerations for others, namely me. It was relatively quiet, with the exception of everyone telling the other one to be quiet or you'll wake-up the sleeping bear. (I heard that!) I'm sure you have been awakened by alarming clocks, chirping birds, crowing roosters and crying babies, but have you ever been roused at 6 a.m. by a fire alarm?

The smoke was dense enough to set-off two alarms at both ends of the house. What a sight to wake up to: a dozen people groggy with sleep and panicked by surprise were running into each other like Keystone Cops. That is everyone but my youngest son, David. He stayed fairly calm because he was the instigator of this early morning panic. There he stood, in his underwear, holding a pair of smoldering pants. He had put them in the kitchen oven to dry, while he unconsciously ate breakfast with smoke circling his sleepy head.

David had this thing with smoke alarms. He had become slightly "shell shocked" after the hot pants incident. A few months later, while taking a steaming shower, he unwittingly set-off a fire alarm with the hot steam. Not knowing the cause, he bounded out of the tub, down the stairs shouting: *"Fire! Fire!"* running at full throttle across the living room.

On occasion, Anne would have the ladies in for a Bible study, or a Tupperware party. Yep! This was one of those days. Wearing nothing but wet skin, the 14-year-old realized his butt was the center of attraction. With his face as red as his rump, he placed one hand in front, and the other behind, and now having a stronger motive than a mere fire, bounded the stairs three at a time, mumbling: *"Man oh man, oh man...!"*

Tell me, how did you rise this morning? With birds singing? A rooster crowing? Have you ever thought about who wakes the rooster on time? I'll tell you who. The Squitieris—that's who. The rooster was heard complaining about early morning wake-up calls. His cock-a-doodle-doo sounded like a painful grunt.

## Smoke Gets in My Eyes

Speaking of birds, smoke, and early morning disruptions. It was a Monday morning, 7 a.m. five hours away from my deadline for Friday's column, and I was having trouble concentrating while sipping my coffee. I was keeping a close eye on my archenemy, my toaster. It had a thing for me: it hated my guts. Yes it did. It made perfect toast every time for everyone but me. It charred mine.

That morning I was sitting there watching the parade of smiling faces go by with perfect, golden, buttered toast. Everyone a masterpiece. I could look out the window and see my last two attempts at making toast in that very same toaster. There they were, smothering in the grass. It's funny, the birds don't come around anymore ever since one died of smoke inhalation. They fly by and stick their tongues out at me. There goes another one. *"Same to you fella! I hope you hit a tree!"* It's a curious thing. I would put the bread in the machine, and stand there and watch it, and while doing so, the smoke would curl around my head. Suddenly, the thing would spit two burning missiles at me. It was definitely out to get me!

My wife says I didn't pay any more attention to the monster then I do her. I took her advice and got as close to the monster as I could (the toaster that is) and stared into both slots. They rushed me to the E.R. for sunburned eyeballs (while my toast burned) Next, I tried setting the shade selector on light. The bread popped-up twice...white. The third time it came up black. I set the dial on very dark hoping it would toast in the first pop. It did...black.

Not one to give up a challenge, I popped the popper every few seconds trying to get the right color. The phone rang...burnt toast. I had the kids tell it the toast was theirs. No good. It knew. It knew. *"Whoes toast is in the toaster?" "It's Dad's!"* answered some fink. **ZAP!** Burnt toast.

One morning I threatened the monster. *"This is your last warning. You burn my bread again and I'll pop your popper and pull your coils!"* Within seconds I had it's answer: two flaming rockets shot into the air one landing in my coffee cup and the other on the kitchen curtain. Obviously trying to get me in trouble with my wife.

I hated the cocamehmeh contraption. I remember one night about midnight, I was watching David Letterman, when suddenly the downstairs smoke alarm went off, and the upstairs followed. Everyone came running down the stairs yelling *"Fire!"* Finally, someone realized I was trying to make toast again. *"Oh Dad...why don't you give-up and have it white!"*

I got back to writing the column, when my eyeglasses fogged-up, and I began to cough...then choke. *"Dad? Are you at the toaster again?"* Yes I said, trying to stay calm as I doused the smoking curtain with my cup of coffee.

## Dohickies, Dingamabobs and Whatchamacallits

We held a memorial service today. A long time friend and family servant had passed on. It was a sad time for most, as we watched the box with the remains being carried out of the house. Some wept, others stood silently watching and remembering the many years of service given by this honorary family member.

It was a slow death. The first sign of weakening was the loss of power. First the left side, then the right. Finally, the dim light of life faded. There were useless efforts by the Turncoats within my walls to save this useless thing.

The family felt a great loss, I did not. Only deep satisfaction and victory. I had out-lived this thing which I had come to hate with a passion. HA! HA! HA!…I had been given the last laugh and had no remorse. Only gladness filled my being, as the rotten, broken carcass was carried out.

Our toaster died today! Good riddance! I'm glad it's gone. While others threw fits of grief, I threw ashes: burnt breadcrumbs the antagonistic monster had left this very morning. Oh how sweet the victory over the croaked piece of junk. *"Yes!"* I shouted, having wonderful feelings of great joy. No longer will I be ingesting smoke, first thing in the morning, and last thing at night. No longer will my toast be white on one side and black on the other. Birds will return to our property, singing gleefully in the trees, no longer losing members of their flock to smoldering discarded toast.

I had purchased a new toaster. One that could be trusted without fear of smoke alarms going off, burning missiles being flung at me while fighting small brush fires. Mmmmmmm! Golden brown toast was on its way. I was gripped with the anticipation of pleasure I would get from the new instrument. When someone asked: *"What's that smell?"* There was something burning…curses, it's the Spirit of Toaster Past!

**TO BEEP OR NOT TO BEEP**

As you can see, my world is a cocamehmeh one filled with whatchamacallits out to try my patience. While the rest of the world is into the Computer Age, I'm still having trouble with toasters that burn, charcoal that doesn't, starters that don't and mowers that won't, unmatchable socks and unlockable locks. By day's end I have such a headache, I need a bottle of aspirin. But even the bottle defies me with its "child proof cap". Not to worry, there are lots of kids around to get it open for me. Who is it they are keeping out of the bottle? Me! That's who!

All is not bleak. I do see a ray of sunshine now and again, tasting the sweetness of victory over inanimate objects that plague me. Last week I had that rare joy. It came through a friend, and his irritating contraption: an answering machine.

Tom is his name. Contracting is his game. Tom spent many days and nights trying to create the perfect name for his remodeling business, discarding dozens that missed the mark.

I called one night to find the gem of a title to be used for his D.B.A.: *"Hello, this is Tom's Home Remodeling…"* Terrific! For this he drained his brain. Can you imagine finding a name for his first born?

I started a conversation with what I thought was Tom, but soon realized Tom was on tape. His Phone-Mate answering machine, like all the rest, is a rude and cold device left behind for friends or telemarketers to visit with while the owner is out, or screening calls. It beeps while you're talking, cuts you off before your done, and in most cases, lies about its owner not being home, while he or she is sneering at your voice.

It's cold, as in mechanical—sans personality or originality. Especially those that use pre-recorded salutations. You know the type, the guy sounds like Orson Wells with a cold: *"Sorry. No one is here to take your call…"* The owner would not take the time to record his own voice, but expects me to do so. Obviously, letter writers they are not.

A disconcerting device to most people, it will first confuse, then intimidate and finally anger the caller, slamming the phone down in disgust. A few desperate souls, will put their shoulders back, clear their throats, and leave overdone or overwrought messages. The trail-offs are interesting:

*"…he's got a dumb answering machine!"* or *"…I don't know if he got the message, it was beeping while I was talking!"* What part of *"Wait for the beep"* don't they understand?

My response to the "bug-a-phone" was: *"Hello little machine. When your daddy gets home, tell him it's terrible the way he leaves you alone without a sitter. You be a good little box and sit there quietly, and don't talk with strange people."* My visit disturbed Tom: *"Speaking of strange people…"* he snapped, *"why are you abusing my machine!"*

I countered with why should I have to talk to a machine, I may as well come over there and talk to your Petunia bush. *"You probably have…"* he said, *"It's been wilting lately!"*

The following day, driven by sheer mischief, I dialed Tom's alter ego. *"Hello Tom's Home Remodeling…"* I was making noises into the phone when I heard Tom say: *"Al it's me!"*

"*Is it you live, or on tape?*" I asked. "*It's me you wacko…*" Tom yelled, "*I caught you red-handed. I'm calling the cops and having you arrested for harassment!*"

"*Are you sure it's you?*" I insisted. While he was still out of control, I left a message: "*This is Al, I'm not here right now, and you are talking to a machine. Continue to make an ass out of yourself since no one is listening! Beep!*

"*Al, I'm having you committed!*" Tom said. To which I replied: "*When you call the asylum, pay no attention to the guy in the background. He thinks he's an answering machine. When asked his name, he says: 'Beep, click!*"

*Hello?...Al?, you screwball!*" Tom yelled……into MY answering machine. **BEEP! BEEP!**

## "No Cost, Just Aggravation"

*"Forget it..."* I told my wife, to an ad selling a desk copier for $99.00. *"what can you get for $99.00?" "But it has a 20-day free trial offer..."* she insisted, *"no cost or obligation, all returns guaranteed, why not?" "No!"* I said. Forcing my authority.

It arrived two weeks later. A tiny thing powered by electricity: a 200-watt light bulb, for crying out load. I reluctantly ran off three poor copies to satisfy Anne, replaced it in the shipping carton, and resealed the top. It was time to test the claim: *"All returns guaranteed!"* Simple, you would think. Sending a man into space and back may be simple...this is a major battle, with the enemy on two fronts.

My first encounter was with the delivery service. The very one who brought the toy, was its designated returner. All I said into the phone was: *"Hello, I have a..."* when the voice cut me off saying: *"Just a minute please, someone will be with you shortly..."* I was put on hold for five minutes, long distance. When that someone returned, I told her if I wanted to spend the morning listening to music, I'd listen to my stereo. She reluctantly apologized and started an interrogation. *"What is the size of the package being picked-up?"* I told her it was the same size as two hours ago. I just wanted it sent back. *"Sir, we must have the size"*. I told her I'd have to call her back. I'm not in the habit of measuring packages I receive in the mail. I called back.

*"The box is 20 inches long, 16 inches wide."* I said, proud of my dexterity with a tape rule. *"How High?"* she asked. *Just a minute…"* I said, holding the receiver under my chin, and manipulating the tape: *"Lets see, it's 12 inches…"* Suddenly the receiver flew across the room. Picking it up I heard, *"…the weight?…what is the weight?"*

I apologized for dropping her on her head, and she merely repeated her question with a grunt: *"The weight, what's the weight?"* What for, I asked, it's the same box going back. Just look-up the size and weight from two hours ago. In a voice sounding like Norma Desmond: *"Sir! Will you PLEASE give me your weight!"* I asked her, why my weight, I wasn't going anywhere, the box was. All I could hear was heavy breathing. I told her breathing in my ear did nothing for me, but it was running up my phone charges. She offered a toll free number and I asked why she hadn't told me sooner, she snapped: *"You didn't ask, SIR!"* I said goodbye, hung-up and called right back.

*"Please hold, someone will be right with you!"* Again, music. This time I didn't mind, it was their dime. When a woman came back on the line, I asked if it was the same person I spoke to before. *"Are you the man without the weight?"* she asked. *"Yes."* I replied. *"Unfortunately, it is I…"* she said. *"Weight?"*

All I said was, I didn't have the weight, and she exploded. I put her on hold, and went after the bathroom scale. It wasn't easy, standing on the scale, holding a 20" X 16" X 12" box while reading the dial out of range of my bi-focal. *"Ahhh…lets see, it's 179 pounds…"* *"What?…"* she cut-in, *"you'll need a trucking company!"*

I told her it was total weight, and I had to deduct myself. *"Sir, put the box on the scale, it would be easier."* *"It doesn't fit the scale..."* I said, *"why don't you just pick it up, that would be easier!"*

*"Let's see, 179 less 170, is 9 pounds. It's 9 pounds!"* She asked its destination and I told her. She said: *"Your package is 20"X 16" X 12", weighs 9 pounds, going to California, the charges are: cost of pick-up, fuel surcharge, delivery charge...oh how much does it cost?"* she asked.

*"I beg your pardon?"* *"It's value..."* she said, *"It must be insured!"* *"It must? why? it's not mine?"* She told me I was responsible for it. *"Oh no I'm not...my wife is!"* I reluctantly told her it was worth about $3.98, but the price tag said $99.00. She said it would be insured for $100, making a grand total of $6.70, payable to the driver. I questioned the charge. It was $2.30 coming here, why was it $4.40 more going back? She ignored my claim. She said it was payable on pick-up or no deal. They were a prepaid service, and my $6.70 was refundable if and when the party accepts the package and charges.

By then the kids were home from school, encircling me as I stood on a scale, holding a box, and shouting. *"What's he doing now?"* one asked. *"Beats me!"* said another, *"...maybe he's going bananas!"* *"Again!"* chirped in the third.

I asked her about the *"If"* and *"when"* and did that mean I may not get my money back. She told me it would take three weeks to find out. Until than, I'm out $6.70.

Two days later they came *right over* to pick up the box, now in a big hurry and laying on his horn. Naturally, going and coming, receiving and billing, took 20 days. I received a bill demanding payment on the piece of junk. I told them the box was sent back weeks ago. I received a phone call asking about its whereabouts. I told him I had sent it back already.

*"Was it Minnesota or California?"* *"California."* *"San Fran or Foster City?"* *"No wonder you lost the box, you move too much!"*

*"Please, Mr. Squitty...Spitteri..."* *"That's Squitieri"* *"Sorry, but we can't locate the package."* I said it was either in San Fran or Foster City, and asked

about my $6.70. He said, he didn't know: *"It was either in San Fran or Foster City!"* Wise guy.

*"Dear..."* my wife said, *"look at this ad: 'raising Chinchillas for fun and profit'...what do you think?...Al?"*

**Slam!**

## A Stitch in Time

*"Dad!...Dad!...wake-up, wake-up!" "Huh?...what?...what's wrong? Is there a fire?" "No! The cat is making funny noises and dragging her legs! I think she broke her back or something!"*

I squinted at my watch: 7 a.m. Sunday. My youngest daughter, Vicky was bouncing on my stomach, trying desperately to get me up—along with last night's dinner.

I looked over at the lump of tightly rolled bed covers next to me. It shifted around and came to rest. *"Did you hear that?"* I asked the motionless mound. *"Mmmmmm..."* it said. *"What do you think?"* I asked. *"Zzzzzz..."* it said *"Thanks..."* I said.

I lifted my excited daughter off my stomach, shook the ringing out of my ear, and followed her downstairs. *"Gracie"* our cat lay belly down, spread eagle on the kitchen floor. I began an examination of the feline as though I knew what I was doing. My knowledge of animals equals that of farming: none.

The kids, bug-eyed, encircled us on the floor. Touching the cat here and there made her whimper. I rubbed her spine and hind legs, which seemed to give some relief. She purred. Marlin Perkins I'm not. Dr.

Doolittle perhaps. We both talk to the animals, but his talk back, while mine walk away.

By that time my Fair Lady was up and moving, ever so slowly. Someone pointed her to the kitchen and stuck a cup of coffee in her hand. She took a sip, opened one eye and asked: *"Is she dead?" "Oh Ma…"* answered Arlene, *"it's not that bad, she's only paralyzed from the hips down!"* WHAT?" screamed Anne, spraying hot coffee over me, six kids and the prone cat. I tried to convince everyone it was only a cramp…or something. My wife insisted upon calling the vet:

*"The poor thing might die. Call the doctor right away!"* I reminded her it was Sunday and it would cost an arm, leg…and at least one kid. *"So what…"* she asked, *"what's more important, the money or the cat?"* Silence fell over the room. *"Well?"* she insisted *"I'm thinking"* I said. *"Don't be funny, just call the vet before the cat croaks!"*

While bundling the ailing feline into the car, I continued my attempt to stay the expense. *"Do you have any idea how much this guy gets? He has the reputation of being the best in the county, and gets well rewarded for the honor!" "So!"* she replied. *"So? I have had a toothache for weeks I can't afford to have it fixed, and you're spending my money on the cat."*

*"Stop yelling, you're scaring the cat!"* she says. I'm scaring the cat! This specialist ranks fourth in income to doctors, lawyers and plumbers, and I'm scaring the cat! Boy was I in trouble. I had just charged him for a plumbing repair job.

We pulled up to his office, which had an attached kennel and a rambling ranch home. The layout covered two country acres and had its own zip code. The weekend nurse had called the doctor and he was walking over. I suggested he use a golf cart. *"Excuse me?"* asked the nurse.

*"Forget it…"* said Anne, *"he's just a little upset!" "Oh, is he worried about the kitty!"* asked the nurse. *"Yea, right!"* said Anne. Giving me her evil eye. Finally, Dr. Livingston appeared: hands deep into his pockets, eyeglasses midway on his nose, and a smirk that said I had just landed on his Boardwalk loaded with hotels.

"Oh, it's the plumber!...Good morning Mr. Plumber!" I told him what I knew about the cat, which took all of 12 seconds. He poked the cat here and there, as I had done. He lifted her up, looked in her eyes, and put her down. Just as I did. He lifted her tail and peeked in...he had me there.

Patting the cat on the head, he asked: *"First cat?" "No I had one other..."* I replied. *"First female cat?"* he clarified. *"Yes!"* I replied. *"It figures!"* he said. I asked if it was serious. *"Not very..."* he said, *"she's in heat!" "Oh..."* I said, feeling like an idiot. No wonder she purred when I rubbed her lower half. I turned to Anne and reminded her about her remark that the cat might die, and that no animal or human had ever died from those symptoms. With ten kids of her own, she was living proof.

*"You should have her fixed!"* butted-in the vet.

*"I beg your pardon?"*

*"I mean the cat!"* he quickly replied. Anne agreed with the doc to have her spayed (the cat)

*"How much?"* I asked. He told us we should get all her shots while we were at it. Anne said that was a good Idea.

*"How much?"* I asked. He said due to a coming holiday, it would take a few extra days, there would be no extra charge for boarding Gracie. Anne thought that was so very nice.

*"How much?"* I asked.

*"Oh, lets say, give or take a few dollars, about $60."*

*"Six...six...sixty dollars?"* I stammered. He said goodbye and walked off leaving Gracie with his assistant. Anne was relieved, and I had an awful pain in my tooth.

Thursday I returned $60 I had charged the doc for his plumbing job and sprang Gracie. When the nurse handed me my receipt, she asked: *"Is there anything wrong?"*

*"Oh no..."* I replied, *"just a toothache."*

*"You should have that fixed right away."* She offered.

*"Yea, right. How's the doc's plumbing holding up?"*

*"Oh, I guess everything is O.K. right now."* she said.

*"Oh, that's too bad!"* I said, rubbing my tooth.

## Freebies in Burgerland

Fast food chains have "Think Tanks" working round the clock finding gimmicks to compete for our business. Regardless of the population, whether it has a large industrial work force, or completely surviving on welfare checks, you will find more than a half dozen indigestion outlets right in the middle of town. Each bragging of faster, cheaper ways to kill us with preservatives, sodium and fat on a sesame seed bun. Regardless of where or what you eat, the "returns" have the same aftertaste.

Drive-thru windows, late store hours, a three part meal for under a buck brings in millions. The reason they know there has been over one billion sold, is because they just finished their first pound of ground beef. One of the gimmicks used to lure housewives—my wife included, are discount coupons. I believe they are as cunning a device as *"Gift Certificates"* given for Christmas or birthdays. My children gave me a total of $150 for Christmas. I went to the mall and purchased men's wear with the gifts: Two suits, one sport coat, and two ties. Good deal. I only had to add $350 to the certificates. I told my family no more certificates, I can't afford their generosity. Likewise, the discount fast food coupon is a clever way of getting families into Heartburn Haven.

Anne found the coupon mixed in with 7 pounds of circulars between six pages of newspaper. Supershopper can spot a 2-for 1 coupon through six inches of lead.

*"Buy one, get one free!"* That makes two, right? Last week, my wife decided to redeem a two-for-one coupon—with me and six kids in the car. Does it say 8 for 1 ? No. Right off we are in deep trouble. The natural question—asked by six screaming kids was: *"Who's getting the two burgers?"* Thankfully, we were only half loaded—with kids that is.

*"Mommy are we eating dinner here?"* asked the youngest. *"No..."* I said, *"we are going home to eat real food, mommy wants to cash in her free coupon. Why now...I don't know."* *"Boy, we never eat out!"* piped in another fast food freak. Last month we made two trips to Burger Prince, three to McDougals, four to the Pizza Rut, and three to Ponda-D-Aroma. That line-up would give the Galloping Gourmet the trots.

We pulled up behind a car loaded with kids. As we waited, a crazed little league mom ordered what seemed like $16.00 worth of Jumboburgers. Then she started the shakes...which became increasingly violent until she took a swig from a brown paper bag. Now stiffened, she ordered the fries, and cokes.

As we waited, the little darlings in front of us were sticking out their tongues, and making weird faces through a catsup stained rear window. Obviously they were there before. We moved up in line. Before our car stopped, a voice came out of the clown's mouth: *"May I have your order please?"* *"Just a minute..."* Anne said, throwing the car into park, *I just got here for crying out loud. let me think!"* *"Your order please!"* the voiced shot back. *"Can't you see I'm reading the menu..."* said Anne, with her head nearly into the clown's mouth. I told Anne she couldn't see us, and she snapped: *"Quite! I'll handle this clown!"*

*"Your order, please!"* begged the voice. *"I'm going to come in there and pull your wires!"* shouted my wife, with the kids cheering her on: *"Give it to her Ma!"*

The cop on the corner started toward us. I told her to calm down and forget the freebie, it's not worth the price of a bail bond. While she insisted it was the clown's fault for rushing her *decision,* I sank slowly under the dashboard.

The voice begged again. *"I'll take one Jumbosaurus, and hold the onions!"* said Anne. *"Hold the what?"* asked the voice. *"What's wrong…"* said Anne, *"your batteries going dead?"* The voice thanked us for the one item order in a strained but polite voice, and said: *"Please move-up!"* Anne informed the voice we could not move up because there was a carload of monkeys in front of us. As we slowly rolled away from the mouth, we heard it say: *"I get all the nuts!"* *"I heard that!"* screamed Anne, hanging out the window.

When we pulled up to the cashier's window, Anne presented the "free" coupon. *"Madam…"* the girl scolded, *"you are suppose to tell us when it's a coupon purchase!""Why?…"* asked Anne, *"will you give me worse service?"* *"Hey Dad the cops here!"*

As we started home, we tired to resolve the clever little problem the 2-for-1 coupon caused: two Jumbosaurus twixt six kids. The solution—cleverly planned by the suits in the Think Tank, worked well. Just *buy* four more.

So Anne makes a U-turn, missing the No U-turn sign, and re-enters the parking lot via a driveway marked Exit Only. The curious cop, obliviously past the end of his 4 p.m. shift, stood with folded arms, shaking is head. As we passed within inches of his flat feet, I smiled. He shook his head at me and blessed himself with the sign of the cross.

As Anne headed for the drive-thru window, I said: *"Oh no you don't…I'll go inside like a normal person. Park the car…carefully!"*

As I walked up to the counter, still reading the overhead menu, an overzealous clone asked; *"Can I help you sir?"* After offering the fact I was a slow reader, a second inpatient pinstriper asked again: *"Can I help you sir?"*

While I waited for my order, a familiar voice flooded the restaurant via the drive-in speaker, *"One free coke…and don't give me any lip!"*

## K-9 Section Eight

In a moment of temporary insanity, my wife and I thought our children needed the companionship of a dog. Most parents have had that thought, which may be nice for those people with two or three lovely, well adjusted children. But a house full of ten kids needs a prissy neurotic poodle, like Noah needed one more day of rain.

We chose a miniature Toy Poodle because anything larger would be a bit overcrowding. The word *"miniature"* was a misnomer. It grew into an 18" *Standard*, and the kennel owner's remark about him being *"just a cute little troublemaker"* was her second understatement. He could have been a stand-in for the M.G.M. lion. Since we pledged to be good poodle owners, we took *"Coco"* to the most expensive veterinarian we could find. Because the Yellow Pages list only those kind, It's just a matter of closing your eyes and randomly pinning-the-tail on any vet.

*"He has fleas, ticks and an ear infection..."* said the Doc, *"He also needs his shots. I'll get him sound as a dollar."* Another underestimate: the dollar

was up to $100 including the kennel and vets visit—and he hadn't been home yet.

To be accepted by the elite Poodle crowd, one is expected to be groomed weekly—the dog that is. I manage an $8.00 haircut twice a year, which—unlike this pampered prissy, doesn't include a bow on my head, little puffs on my feet, or a ball on my tail. And his trim is $24 a salon visit, including bath and perfume.

These visits to the Dog Lady, whom he hated, may have contributed to Coco's drastic personality change. I believe this undignified sissy treatment of pomp, puff and powder, turned an already eccentric poodle into a psychotic canine. For days after the clipping, he'd hide his near naked body under my bed, gnashing his teeth and gnarling at everything that came near.

He became a growling beast which nail polish and pink bows did nothing to hide. He bit into brooms, vacuum cleaner hose, bicycle tires and 31 assorted arms, feet and legs, be they attached to human or furniture. Since the Mad Dog had never bitten me, the daily casualty reports were hard to understand: *"Coco bit the mailman, the milkman, the paper boy and the garbage truck."* I was sure it wasn't Coco's fault. Obviously the mailman sprayed him, the milkman kicked him, and the paperboy beaned him. He bites our kids because they annoy him. I'd like to bite them myself. As for the garbage men—ditto! It's the flinging of trashcans and lids over my front yard that irritates both of us.

Coco ruled by intimidation. If he were eating on the front porch, the kids used the back door. My wife never vacuumed while he was napping, claiming the high cost of hose replacements, rather than the fear of the beast. Friends and relatives knowing of Coco's hatred of the doorbell, always tapped lightly, and refused to enter not knowing his whereabouts.

We once tried to use him as a "stud" with a friend's insistence. We begged him to change his mind since we had no idea what the off-spring would be like and felt one Coco roaming God's good earth was more than enough. But the owner of this pleasant, gentle poodle won out and the blind date was arranged.

Coco had no idea of the arrangements. He was shoved, snarling into a pantry, and in a few minutes, the perfumed Deb was pushed in to meet him. It was fright at first sight.

Instead of groans and moans of pleasure, there was growling and gnashing of teeth coming from Coco; and sorrowful whining from the rejected prissy. As she came running out of the love nest, Coco was right on her tail…literally. The friend asked what was Coco's problem, and I said I didn't know, either he had a headache, or seriously feared commitments.

Then the final bite. We had to take a trip and I made the dumb decision to bring the carnivore. The pills the vet gave Coco to calm him, worked in reverse. It was like putting "uppers" in King Kong's bananas. He chewed the road map, upholstery, rear view mirror and the kids. Arlene has mementos on her arm.

We stopped the pills, putting Coco in a comatose state. His glazed eyes stared into space, and his tongue dangled its full length. Ours minds were made up, Coco the Killer Mutt had to go, and quickly before his next fit.

I stopped at a "service" station—one of those use-to-be places that once gave you service, and asked to use their phone. The attendant overheard me say to a veterinarian that I had a mentally disturbed poodle I wanted to put "nite-nite" quickly. The attendant offered to buy the neurotic poodle, insisting it would be a shame to put such an expensive dog to sleep. He thought it would make a great companion for his mother, living alone in a mobile home park. I told him the man-eater was unsafe and not for sale. But he persisted and finally won the argument, but with one stipulation: I had him sign a waver, releasing me from any future damages caused by Coco, to the mobile, furniture or his mother. Ha!, he laughed, insisting that was no problem. He offered to pay for the psychotic, but I refused the money. That would be like charging a condemned man for the firing squad bullets. No I told him, save the money for more important things like furniture and doctors.

Months later we stopped back at the station to inquire about CoCo. *"Oh, he's gone…"* the man said, *"he bit my mother; the mailman and for some unknown reason, the Avon lady!"*

We asked his whereabouts, and he said he didn't know. The last he heard, he was given to an elderly couple at an RV campground. But he hadn't seen them since.

Keep an eye open, folks. If you see an apricot-colored poodle dragging an RV, stay clear. Don't let those pink bows fool you. It may be that cute little troublemaker, Coco the Carnivorous Canine.

## Blooming Blunder Awards

On occasion, I rewarded my readers with Blooming Blunder Awards for real life happenings that in themselves describe the reason for the so-named booby prize. It was satisfying knowing there were a handful of people who were at least as dumb as me.

*"Hero: A person who performs a brave or noble act"*

This months B.B. goes to my brother-in-law, husband to my youngest sister. A horror movie nut who becomes comatose watching a "B" movie. His concentration is so intense, an Elk can pass through his gaze undetected, in fact, the whole Club's Membership can walk through his living room unnoticed. This particular Saturday night may help cure him of his obsession.

His wife had put their two boys to bed and like the moose, she went unnoticed next to him on the sofa. The late movie had him on the edge of his mind, gawking at the screen. The house was dark, with only the glare from the One-eyed Beast.

He had eaten two pizzas, drank three cokes, and gnawed ten fingernails watching the stupendous thriller: *"The Behemoth Grease Ant that Swallowed the Piggy Wiggy Spare Rib Chain."* Their youngest son, awakened by a bad dream, settled on the sofa 'twixt engulfed father and bored-to-no end mother.

Suddenly, the boy let out a blood-curdling scream that sent both parents bolt upright against the wall.

*"Daddy, daddy it's coming, there's a giant spider, it's coming after us!"* The boy's Dad tried to assure him it wasn't a giant spider, but an ant. *"No Daddy, not on the TV, it's under the hassock…there, it's crawling toward us!"*

*"Get down and kill it!"* shouted his wife, prying him from the wallpaper.

*"Don't move…"* he said, *"I'll get a broom and kill it!"*

It was the size of a softball. Black with furry arms. The dim light of the TV gave it an ominous appearance. He returned with the broom and said:

*"Shhh, I'm going to smash it, don't make a sound!"*

The only sound that could be heard was the synchronized knocking of three pairs of knees. He reached down and slowly moved the hassock, exposing the creature. He raised the weapon, and with quick fierce movements, brought it down again and again with great force, knocking the table lamp to the floor. He swung feverishly with tremendous speed, the updraft fluttering picture frames on the wall. With eyes wide, and changing expressions of fear and anger, he pounded the thing motionless.

Exhausted, perspiring and shaken, he had protected his family. Lowering himself to the floor, he poked it with the broom handle, which he had splinted in the battle. His wife replaced the lamp and turned it on. He moved closer to the flattened thing. He killed it. A large, black lump of woolly **KNITTING YARN!** My brother-in-law. Some kind of hero! (?)

## BLOOMING BLUNDER AWARD

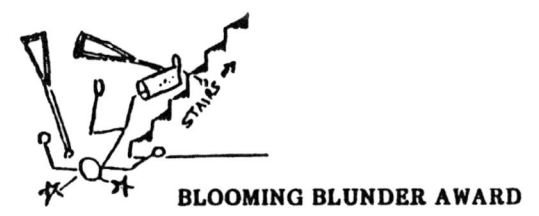

My son-in-law has been on crutches for eight weeks. He managed to survive a 14 foot fall at the plant where he works, but two weeks later he broke his foot in another mishap. The dictionary calls an awkward person a *"klutz"*, but you wouldn't think just because he had two near misses, that term would fit him...but, what if he had a third chance at killing himself just eight weeks later?

Have you ever tried walking on crutches? It is not an innate ability, and takes some getting use to. He has learned to handle them with some dexterity, but in the beginning the going was tough, and near misses were plentiful.

After sitting around the house with nothing to do for the first two weeks, he became bored. After all, he could only eat, watch TV, eat, sleep, and eat, all of which becomes a drag on the brain, to say nothing of the posterior.

One morning he decided to surprise his wife by bringing in the mail. He managed to get down the 100-foot ice and snow covered driveway, and getting the mail out of the box, which sat back from, and behind a five-foot snow bank.

While he stood in the road looking through his mail, he heard a loud rumbling noise. When he looked up, he saw the *"world's largest, fastest"* snowplow coming at him.

He grabbed his crutches and started for the driveway, screaming at the smirking plow driver. It was useless.

There is a point system used by plow drivers: mailboxes are worth 10 points, dogs are 20, parked cars 50 (but only rear or front bumpers, the whole car doesn't count) little old ladies are 75, with an extra five points if on a walker. There are no points given for filling in driveways, unless the guy is still shoveling. But the Big One is a guy on crutches.

He fell into the driveway face first in the snow. He laid there shaking his crutch at the plow driver, who went merrily rolling down the road tearing up lawns, knocking down mailboxes, and chasing dogs, cats and people out of the road.

He did exactly what he started out to do: surprise his wife with the mail. *"How did you get the mail? and how did you get it all wet?"* his wife asked. *"Believe me,"* he replied, *"it wasn't easy!"*

He also found going downstairs can be as dangerous as out running the Yellow Baron of the Highways. It can be awkward and dangerous until you learn the procedure, and there is a defined procedure for getting down stairs with crutches.

First, you place the crutches on the next lower step. Then, you lower your body to the waiting crutches, put there before you leave the step you are standing on.

He got a little confused and reversed the procedure.

After all, he hadn't been himself lately, and his mind was a little boggled, why with falling down twice and knocking himself out, and narrowly missing a one hundred pointer with the plow, he was a little out of touch.

He lowered his foot *first*, leaving the crutches and his shoulders up on the last step. This maneuver puts the body in an unbalanced position: it leans the upper body forward. He knew he was in deep trouble right away. He reacted immediately"

*"HELP!"*

It wasn't too bad. There were eight steps going down for him to bounce off, but he missed every one of them. He landed on his head…again.

We keep him tied-up now. His chair faces the TV, and the ropes aren't too tight. We spoon-feed him every four hours, which is upsetting to him since it limits his intake.

With close observation, we should be able to keep him out of a body cast. He isn't allowed to use stairs or get the mail, and if necessary, we will confiscate his crutches.

## "ANOTHER BLOOMING BLUNDERER BESTOWED"

As followers of my column know, occasionally I reward a deserving person the non-coveted award for a blooming blunder. My choice of recipient has always been non-biased and without much attention to personage, office and/or title. Winners may be found anywhere this column appears, so keep a low profile…and your head down. Everyone is fair game.

A few of the Past deserving blunderers have been: my brother-in-law the knitting yawn warrior, my son-in-law the klutz on Krutches and least we forget, my editor, the Midol popping managing editor of this newspaper, who, a bit overworked and seriously forgetful, drove his car for months ignoring the red light on his dashboard. The "annoying" red light went out when David replaced his car engine. Because of that, we forgave him for missing the dinner date at our house, which he remembered three days later.

This month's award goes to the Honorable County Court Judge of Oswego County New York.

The qualifying story took place when five married couples took a camping trip into the Cranberry Lake area of the Adirondacks, northeast of Watertown, N.Y. They canoed or went canoeing, up the Oswegathie River (don't ask me, I just write this stuff) After paddling for seven miles they stopped to set-up camp…naturally, coming ashore first.

Full fledged outdoorsmen, and ladies, they chose to pitch a tent in the damp, chilly night air, rather than use a comfortable cabin, or my own choice: a motel room.

Our protagonist, better known as *"Wally"* was thoughtful to purchase a new coffeepot. Nothing fancy, just an agate pot to boil coffee over the open flame the way the cowboys did in the ol' west. They gathered sticks, made a fire, and then gathered round in a circle for dinner and a good cup of hot coffee. *"Good coffee Wally!"* patronized a male camper. *"Ya, it has that deep, dark color..."* added another.

*"Oh my..."* gasp a female camper, *"no wonder they died with their boots on"*

*"Is this what made them rough and tough cowhands?"* questioned her counterpart, shaking her head while swallowing.

*"No...this is what made them mean and nasty!"*

The men told the woman to pipe down and quit complaining, they were suppose to be *"roughin' it!"* and all agreed it was a long day and retired into their sleeping bags for the night.

Wally was up at the crack of dawn and put the pot on.

*"Hey Wally, making some of your good strong java?"*

*"Sho-nuf!"* mimicked the Judge, *"Be ready in the shake of a skunks tail!"*

*"It smells like the skunks been here and gone"* said his wife Betty, *"it sure smells strong!"*

Our winner, doubting his wife's ability to know good coffee when she smells it, stuck his nose into the hot pot. Opening the lid, he mused: *"Son-of-a-gun! So that's were I packed them things. I knew I'd find them there in the new pot."*

*"Find what?"* asked a woodsman, sipping his fresh coffee. *"Theses..."* answered Wally, lifting dripping brown socks from the coffeepot.

*"UGH!"* yelled the man, dropping his cup and spraying his mouthful on everyone.

*"Yuck!"* exclaimed Betty, clutching her throat. *"Wally's socks, for heaven's sake—of all things...his socks!"*

*"Calm down, calm down..."* insisted the Judge, *"they're clean socks, I packed them straight from the laundry!"*

No one got sick from the deep dark brown coffee the Judge had served-up, but the Judge was limited to simple chores of gathering wood, and washing his socks…down by the stream, far from the cooking fire.

Congratulations Your Honor, the honor is deserved.

(*P.S. A true story. Color has been added to give it body.*)

## I Goof...You Blunder

Family, friends and readers ask why I haven't received one of my Blooming Blunder Awards. My repeated answer to so many seemingly vicious inquires is simple: I haven't made any! On the other hand, I haven't scratched the surface when it comes to my family's blunders. I can fill pages, but it wouldn't be fair since I have the advantage writing this column.

(*Spouse and offspring are reading this as I write and are demanding equal time, which is out of the question!*)

Where was I? Oh yes, I could tell about the time my daughter Lorraine, then a college student studying to be a nurse, took her temperature with the thermometer wrong end out. Or the time she cutout an entire dress pattern with her three fingers squeezed through the smaller hole of the scissors. (*Here comes my wife back again with the vacuum cleaner...No!*

*get your own column, I'm not saying that!*)

It wouldn't be fair to tell readers about my son-in-law mistakenly using the ladies room in a crowded restaurant, than telling his wife to get out after she told him so. Or the time he scared himself while looking into a full-length mirror behind a bathroom door, thinking someone was hiding there.

Likewise, it would be unfair to mention the time Arlene, trying to avoid embarrassment, stood quietly choking to death on a button. Why a twenty-year old would suck on a button, is still unclear. Adding injure to insult, her sister Danielle, after whacking her on the back and dislodging the object, got reprimanded by the ungrateful near dead.

"*You hit me too hard!*" she complained. Danielle warned. "*Well next time choke to death and see how you like it!*"

My family insists I admit those goofs and blunders I may have made, but for the life of me I can't recall any.

(*Here's that woman again with a feather duster…What?…oh alright I'll mention that one, if you'll leave me alone!*)

Once upon a time (*and only this once!*) I made a blunder. But mind you it wasn't my fault. I was driving between calls when I suddenly had a strong uncontrollable urge to use a public restroom. I found one behind a mini-mart gas station. Rushing into the men's room, I slammed the door behind me and soon realized a touch of heavenly bliss and relief.

When I turned to leave, I noticed the doorknob missing from the door. There was a hole where the knob should be. It quickly became apparent that I was trapped in that porcelain and steel walled prison, with its unique and over-powering odor.

Unsuccessfully, I tried pulling the door open with the tip of my finger in the knobless hole. I tried pulling on the crack between the door and its casing, breaking two of my finest fingernails, now leaving me with ten bad ones. In the course of the 45 minute attempted escape, I also broke two pencils, a PaperMate and four teeth out of my comb.

Considering the seemingly hopeless situation, I stayed relatively calm—even when my finger got stuck in the hole. There were no signs of panic or claustrophobia, just perspiration and a mild quiver, the kind I get when I'm near a mother-to-be having one-minute contractions.

Thinking I may faint away, I started doing what anyone would do in this situation: I started pounding and kicking the door, while screaming "**HELP!**"…

Amazingly the place was swarming with people buying gas and walking to and from the mini-mart, but not a soul heard me banging, bellowing and bawling from frustration. Sinking down onto the porcelain throne and deeper into despair, I began to imagine the newspaper headlines:

*"Columnist found dead in a service station restroom. Authorities puzzled by the cause of death, say it may have been asphyxiation. Confusing was the fact the police had to dislodge the victim's finger from a keyhole. The writer's wife said it may have been days, but being preoccupied with their ten children and daily trips to the mall, she never missed him."*

Miraculously, as I prayed for mercy and dedicated my life to helping incarcerated prisoners, the door popped open allowing me another chance at life. As I walked to my car, enjoying the clean, fresh air of freedom, I passed a man rushing to the rest room. He said a quick "*Hi!*" and kept running. I returned the salutation with: *"Have a nice stay!"* (Isn't it sinful the way we forget those holy vows made when applying our Foxhole Religion.)

I hope this satisfies those who have pestered me about this sort of admission…(*Oh, she's back again! What story? No I'm not telling that one. I'm out of space. Maybe next column.*)

"*Did you hear about the time Al…*" (now cut that out!)

## "Them" is a Fighting Word

Today's column is for men only. All ladies please leave the room. (Have they gone yet? I don't want *them* to hear this.)

I have just been called a Male Chauvinist and don't know why.

I think it may have started over grocery shopping, something I dislike even more than browsing in department stores without money. My lady makes me do it.

Not a comparative shopper myself, I'm boggled by the sight of a housewife blocking the aisle while she feverishly checks differences betwixt sale items and generic products. She will divide ounces into pounds, cents into dollars and whatever goes on during this session of high finance. But don't confuse her with the cost of a gallon of gas or M.P.G., when she drives cross-town to save a dime on toilet paper. Besides, I'm sure her husband knows the cost of groceries and gave her more than enough to cover the tab. Right fellas?

My wife never has a shortage problem with cash. She asks for a twenty-dollar bill when she only needs five bucks. She calls it *"just-in-case money"* which in this case, I never see again.

When I shop with Anne she never lets me help. I put brand "A" in the cart and she replaces it with brand "X". She scolds me publicly for impetuously grabbing just any box of salt. **SALT!**

When I shop alone I'm cool. I move swiftly down the aisles throwing items into the cart. Occasionally I misjudge the register tab. But one learns to sacrifice life's necessities and the canned shrimp, frozen lobster and caviar go back.

Yesterday she gave me a list and sent me into the "war zone" with these orders: *"Get a **nice** head of lettuce, some **nice** tomatoes and a **nice** onion."* Then she added: *"Watch the prices!"* Pray tell, guys, what is a "**nice head**"? or a "**nice tomato**" ? On a street corner I'd know what they refer to, but a "**nice onion**"?

I managed a nice parking space, found a nice cart and picked some nice veggies. While choosing from a nice array of cold meats, a woman brazenly reached into my cart and squeezed my tomatoes! *"Nice!...*she said, *"some nice tomatoes!"* Imagine a perfectly strange woman—well, maybe not perfect...

Leaving the deli-counter, I edged into traffic where shopping carts move at speeds of up 40 miles per hour. I watched an impregnated woman zoom down the soap aisle discarding expired coupons. She was pushing the cart with her "drum" while dragging two Elves either side of the wagon. One little guy was crying as he tried keeping up, since his finger was caught in the cart. His red-faced Ma, with a pencil gripped between her teeth, and hair dangling over one eye—was saying: *"If you don't shut-up, I'll give you something to cry about!"* What could be worse than being dragged by a crazed pregnant driver.

Another common annoyance: parking loaded carts mid-aisle while conversing.

"Did ja hear about Ida?"

"Ya, she ran-off with the insurance man, and Marvin still warm da ashes!"

"I should be so lucky! Two Hundred Thousand he left!" "Not 'her' he didn't left, 'them' he left 200,000!"

"Oh ladies..." I interrupted, "can I get through here!" "So get threw awreddy, who's stopping you?" said one.

"Boy! some peoples got the noyve!" said da utter one.

At the checkout I found a full unattended wagon. The cashier was leaning against the register chewing gum and filing her fingernails. When she looked up, she signaled me to come around the loaded wagon. I refused. She gestured again. I refused. Under that uniform she is one of *"them"*, and is suspect like the Indian scout wearing a Calvary hat...with a feather! Whose side is she on? It could be an ambush, with the missing shopper jumping out and battering me with a stick of pepperoni.

Slipping through the *Ten Item Express Line* with eleven items brought some strange stares. At first I thought they were envious of my *"nice"* buys, until a woman in her late 90's threatened me with her umbrella: *"What's wrong sonny, can't you count?"* I leaned her back on her walker, paid my bill and ran.

I finally got home and placed the shopping on the table. *"Where's the beef?"* Anne asked.

*"I have to go back? —Please, please not twice in one day, I'll get battle fatigue!"*

"You're complaining..." she snapped, *"I'm there everyday!"*

"Yes, but you're one of 'them'.." I said.

"What do you mean, I'm one of 'them'?" Anne asked.

"Well, you know what I mean, one of those housewives!"

"You male chauvinist!" she yelled.

I ask you, gentleman, after hearing all the facts, what did I say wrong? I mean name one thing!

Boy...women!...go figure.

## Embarrassing Moments

We all have had them. Those face-reddening goofs and blunders we make while someone is watching. Like the tree falling in the forest, it is only noticed if someone is present. The greater the crowd, the brighter the flush.

Bad things, it is said, come in threes. But all in one day? My first red-faced incident came at a department store when I tried to help a female shopper on with her coat. As I pulled it over her shoulders, I stuck my finger in her eye. She walked out with a red eyeball, and I was left with a saleswoman's glare.

While hiding in the toy aisle waiting for my flush to leave my face, my daughter handed me a toy viewer with really neat Mickey Mouse slides. Awe-struck by the 3-D pictures of *"Mickey & Friends"*, I babbled out load about each character as I snapped the viewer held up to my face. After a few moments of enjoyment, I lowered the toy to speak to my daughter, who unbeknown to me, split. In her place stood an elderly woman starring at me and shaking her head in disbelief. Pointing to the viewer, I made a feeble attempt at an explanation: *"Goofy!"* I said.

*"You sure are!"* she snarled.

## A Flight in Shivering Armor

*"It was a cold and windy day"* (hackneyed, but true) when we left the department store with two strikes of embarrassing stupidity against me. With daughter and son at my side, we watched a large woman waddling along an ice-glazed sidewalk, step gingerly from the curb onto the street.

"**CRASH!**" The woman went down like the Titanic, listing aft. Ice fell from power lines as the after shock registered 6 on the Rector Scale, giving unsuspecting shoppers a jolt. With all due respect, she was a large woman…a VERY large woman.

She sat teetering awkwardly on the frozen pavement amid Christmas packages, her hat down over her eyes, graphically cursing the city's D.P.W. and His Honor the Mayor.

*"Don't move, I'll get you!"* I shouted, springing into action—the way I do when Anne is having a baby. Leaving my children at the curb, I took my first…and only step onto the street. My gallant charge ended with an embarrassing thud. As I sped to her rescue with both of my feet in the air, she raised her arms in defense and screamed, *"Oh my God, he's coming at me!"* The amused crowd grew in number from my first step onto the ice. We juggled each other, reminiscent of an old Laurel and Hardy movie: Her Oliver, and yours truly…the skinny one.

*"That's my Daddy helping that fat lady!"* said my proud son. *"No it isn't!"* countered my embarrassed daughter, slapping her brother's hat off his head.

While the laughing rubberneckers looked on, she managed to lift her 300 + pounds off my flattened body. She looked down and held her hand out. *"Here Sir Galahad, let me help you up!"*

As we parted company through the hysterical crowd, she shouted back at me *"Hey Sir Knight…the next time you see me in the gutter, please, leave me there!"*

To which the crowd gave a rousing cheer!

# I Get Letters…Lots of Letters

I also get phone calls and people-on-the-street comments. Some are legit, earnest questions. Others are silly comments in jest. I'm no Dear Abby or Dear Al or any kind of Dear. All letters and comments are answered in like manner as they are asked. Here forthwith are a few:

Q. *Dear Al: We are planning to take our large family out to dinner. We are eight in all. Since you have ten kids, we want to know if you have any suggestions for a quick, inexpensive, and inconspicuous dinning?*

A. Yes. A bucket of KFC, deep in the woods.

Q. *Dear Al: Being a father of ten, what do you do when your child refuses to take a bath?*

A. Use Lysol on the Rug Rat. He'll beg for soap and water.

Q. *Dear Al: I have seen you and several of your children. They are all beautiful. Your wife must be the good looking one!"*

A. Same to you lady!

Q. *Dear Al: You say you'll keep your wife around for a while. Seems to me after what I read, you had better ask her.*

A. Who asked for your opinion!

**Q.** *Mr. Squitieri: Do you really have such a wacky family? If so, I would not mind having dinner at your house. Must be fun!*

**A.** Oh yes, you'll do just fine!

**Q.** *Dear Al: What makes you say wives are always spending money without concern. I'm indignant!*

**A.** Right. And your husband's in debt.

**Q.** *Mr. Squitieri: Why are you always picking on nurses?*

**A.** Did you hear the one that goes: *"You are entering the Quiet Zone of this hospital. Please try not to make any nurse!"*

**Q.** *Dear Al: Can you name your ten children?*

**A.** Sure. Lets see, there's Jimmy…What? I don't have a Jimmy? Then who's that eating at my house every night?

**Q.** *Dear Al: You play with dialects and language, can you write something in Spanish?*

**A.** "Jes!"

**Q.** *Dear Mr. Squitieri: My brother and I are having an argument over who made the best President: Nixon or Clinton?*

**A.** Lee Iacocca; Tommy Losurdo V.P. Pat Copper Speaker.

**Q.** *Dear Al: I read were you are from New York City. I'm from the Bronx, near the Zoo. How about you?*

**A.** No, I never lived near the Zoo, unless they've built a fence around East Harlem.

**Q.** *Dear Mr. Squitieri: Why does a grown man fight with toasters and answering machines?*

**A.** They started it!

**Q.** *Dear Al: Why do you dislike Rap and Hard Rock music?*

**A.** Music? You mean that mumbling and jive set to noise!

**Q.** *Dear Al: What is your definition of a Henpecked husband?*

**A.** One that would rather switch than fight.

**Q.** *Dear Al: Would you say marriage is a 50/50 proposition?*

**A.** No. It's 100 %: One half the time the wife is right, and the other half the time the husband is wrong.

**Q.** *Dear Al: Do you really believe there is such a thing as a Henpecked husband?*

**A.** There were two lines at St. Pete's Gate. 100 men stood on the line marked; *"Henpecked"* One lone man stood in the line marked: *"Nonconformist"*. When St. Pete saw him, he asked him why he was standing there? He answered: *"My wife told me to!"*

**...On Writing**

**Q.** *Al: Where do you get your ideas every week? Do you ever run out of things to say?*

**A.** _____?

**Q.** *Dear Al: Are your funny stories true?*

**A.** Truth is funnier than fiction. If you can sense the comic within the tragic, add exaggeration and write it right.

**Q.** *Al: Are you considered a reporter or writer?*

**A.** The contrast is similar to a photographer and an artist.

One captures reality, the other something from nothing.

**Q.** *What are Tautologies?*

**A.** When you write remember: *advanced planning* is *important* and *relevant*. Be *absolutely sure* when your piece is *all complete,* that you haven't used that *extra plus* on *each* and *every* line. I offer that in genuine sincerity.

**Q.** *Al when will you stop publishing these dum...*

**A.** Now...

**Q.** *Dear Al: What is your best piece of advice to writers?*

**A.** Keep it lean, and know when to quit...Ciao!

## I Also Write Letters...

Dear Son:

This is an answer to your question written in my Birthday Card: *"Dad how does it feel to be 50?"*

**"DEAR DAD: HOW DOES IT FEEL TO BE 50?"**

It was funny you should ask just that day. I was recalling my 45th birthday and what my thoughts were back then, just five years before. I was invited to sub for a player at a game of slow-pitch softball. I was feeling kind of old that day since I had retired the glove five years before at 40.

As you may know, your Pop was a pretty good ballplayer in his youth. I played "stickball" on the streets of New York, and the original "sandlot" on empty lots where buildings once stood. Sliding on rubble brought cuts and bruisers but lots of fun. As in life: we mixed pain with joy.

Softball and Hardball came with age. By ten I was playing on three teams, and changing "jerseys" three times per day. The uniform was actually a Tee shirt and cap either sponsored by a local business or put together with our own pennies. That is until you made the P.A.L. team (Police Athletic

League) than you wore a real uniform made from 100% wool. Baseball being a summer sport, we wondered what were the organizers thinking?

I kept that up till I met your Mom, than I slowed it down to a few games per week of softball. When I hung-up the spikes five years before, it was tough. It meant facing a fact of life: I was getting older and there were things I couldn't do any longer. On that list, was playing ball.

My last year of softball was showing signs of slowing down. I had 42 singles and one triple. The amount of "one baggers" worried me, and the triple should have been an in the park Home run. Only God knows what it took to reach third base.

Just the same, I went to practice that day. We played a scrimmage to loosen-up. But I didn't get loose. In my mind's eye, I was running the bases at full speed, diving for hot grounders, hitting the long ball, but in reality son, I could barely make first base on a weak grounder. I thought maybe I could train and get into some kind of shape, but was it worth the pain?

The hustle had left my legs. The good hitting-eye had dimmed, and the bi-focal didn't work on pop flies. I convinced the manager that the last stop for old-timers was in the green pasture of right field. The infield is for the young and quick, like yourself and your brothers. My arm, which once pitched a 27 and 3-baseball season, could barely hit the cut-off man.

It was a discouraging day, son, realizing there was something you did and loved all your life that you could not do any longer. Things you did at 25 that were impossible at 45. You know your Dad: if he can't do it well, he won't do it at all.

So I passed on the invite. The older guys who still see themselves as young kids, will not accept the inevitable. Instead, they lose work due to sprained muscles and broken bones. And who feeds the family when insurance doesn't cover childish whims?

When they tell me it's just for the fun of it—while stuck on the sofa with a cast, I think I'd rather do what I'm doing for a hobby: writing. And from the size of my acceptance checks, it is for the fun of it. But if I make a reader smile, it's fun.

That's the key, kid, fun. Don't ever do something you dislike to please someone else. Don't go to school to please me or your mom. Don't take a job simply for the money, but because it is something you will enjoy doing. If not, like your dad after thirty years of plumbing, you won't be happy with just the money. Remember these three axioms I have drilled into you kids:

**One:** *It is better to try—and fail, then to fail to try.*
**Two:** *Talent is a gift, one you did nothing to receive. Use it.*
**Three:** *Blest is the man who uses his God given talent to earn a good living while enjoying his work. That is contentment.*

How does it feel to be 50? The same as yesterday at 49, but the mile marker tells me the road is running out and I should make the best of whatever time He has left for me. Tomorrow becomes yesterday much too soon, so don't waste precious time. That someday we talk about, will be here and gone in the twinkling of an eye.

I will add one more item to that important list of three: I will love all ten precious Pearls no matter what you are or become. Remember, God the Father loves you unconditional, and so will I…now and for eternity.

"Your Old Man"

# Absence Makes the Heartburn Stronger

Anne Squitieri (and children)
Cabin On the Lake
Upstate New York

My Dearest Wife:
It seems like months since the plane you were on flew out of sight. but I'm told it has been only two weeks.

When are you coming home?

I hope you and the kids are having a nice vacation. The two girls and I are managing. There isn't much to do evenings. TV has reruns, Info commercials and political ads. It's getting harder to tell one from another.

Dinnertime is unusually calm with just three of us at the table. There is less jerking of dishes and fork stabbing. Arlene handles meals fairly well. We have a hot meal occasionally, like macaroni and cheese (three times this week) and the Campbell people have an amazing red-label variety. I think my blood pressure is up. Could it be too much salt?

When are you coming home?

We had a mishap yesterday. Arlene set the crock-pot on automatic before we left for work. When we got home, we found an awful smell in the kitchen. Danielle said she never heard Arlene telling her to add water to the lentils and stir regularly. Danielle said it was 7 a.m. and she was fast asleep. We settled for hot dogs. Arlene boiled a Family Pak of 12. I suppose it will take a while to eat them up. More salt.

When are you coming home?

Arlene makes interesting lunches for everyone. There is a new surprise everyday: One day one slice wheat, one white. Two slices of ham, one cheese…no bread. Sometimes she breaks it up: two bread, no meat. Two cheese, two bread, no mustard. One day I found a beautiful red apple. Period.

When are you coming home?

Have you ever heard of Chuckwagon Burgers or something like that? Arlene made some last week. They were a bright orange when they went into the oven, and came out the same color. Aren't they suppose to do something in there? Well, Danielle had peanut butter and jelly and I a ham and cheese, on two slices of bread.

Well Arlene started crying and yelling something about Lincoln freed the slaves and Julia Child didn't have to cook for us! She was saying we didn't appreciate her. She said: *"I work all day and than come home to slave over a toaster oven! The least you can do is eat and not gag in front of me!"*

All Danielle said was: *"Okay.. we'll throw-up behind your back!"* and Arlene lost it, *" MAW! When are you coming home!"*

It seems nothing is going right since you flew off into the blue. I ran out of gas on the way home *with your car*, and walked in a Florida monsoon—which fell only on my side of the street. The next day I had a flat—*with your car*. I realize you need room in your trunk, and the dumb spare is in your way. Since you keep the spare in the garage, I had to buy a $20 used tire from a near-by junk dealer. I don't mind the price of the tire, but his junk yard dog tore my pants. In the seat!

How are the grandkids? I'll bet they are hugging and kissing you and telling you how much they love you. It's good for them to remember at least one of their grandparents. If I should come to mind, say *"Hi"* for me.

Well I guess I had better close this letter, dinner is done, the smoke alarm went off. Boy that thing is loud. I think I'll kill it tomorrow, right after I kill the toaster oven.

I don't know what it is we are having, but I'm sure it will be a surprise. I sure appreciate you.

When are you coming home?

Love,

Your Pillar of Salt

Postmark: Clearwater

## Good Ol' Southern Hostility

We have just moved back to New York State from Florida, and yes, we had a nice trip thank you. We just added 3,000 miles to our odometer and did it without car trouble, accidents or tickets. The forgoing due mainly to my being a good mechanic, careful driver and a law-abiding citizen. That remark, for some unknown reason to me causes my wife to laugh hysterically. I suppose she is thinking about that minor misfortune we had in South Carolina. It really wasn't anything at all.

We were moving along at the required "double nickels" (well maybe three quarters) hauling our 16 foot tandem trailer behind our fully loaded, full sized station wagon.

We came up behind an MG sports coup, when a police car mysteriously appeared from out of nowhere and pulled alongside.

He stayed there a very long time. He would fall back, and come along side again. All the while sneering into our car. What was just as strange was the fact he was wearing his ten gallon Stetson in his cruiser.

It became uncomfortable, with him lingering to my left, the MG gaining on my front end, a semi-trailer getting pushy at "my back door" and Anne repeating: *"You're getting too close…you're getting too close!"* as If I didn't already know that!

The two young men in the red MG, intimidated by the trooper, slowed to about 50. With the MG's ski rack tickling my grille work, and Anne working up a foam, I had to act fast. The trooper had fallen back out of view, so I made my move. As I pulled out into the passing lane, my son Christopher leaned forward and asked: *"Dad, what's that trooper doing?"*

*"Why do you kids talk to me when I'm in a driving situation!"* still preoccupied with passing and trying to haul-in this fish tailing barracuda.

*"That one over there, in the middle!"* he insisted.

South Carolina's answer to Duke Wayne was bouncing and swerving uncontrollably down the medium. He had a death grip on the steering wheel, eyes big as saucers, and a glowing red face.

His Stetson was crushed down over his ears and his silver-coated sunglasses dangled loosely under his nose.

As I merged right, landing the fish in the right lane, The Duke swerved wildly back onto the pavement and back alongside. *"Pull that car over!"* (vulgarity deleted)

He jumped out of his car before it stopped rolling, as dozens of motorists slowed to rubberneck. He screamed at me:

*What the——do you think you're doing?"* I calmly asked: *"Did I do something wrong officer?"*

*"What!"* he yelled, *" You jackass, you run me off the——road with that——*
*——fish tailing monster!"* I'm thinking this man has a very limited vocabulary. I merely asked about his loitering and starring, as if we were freaks, and it sparked another torrid rage. Meanwhile my wife, fearful I'd get excited and than shot, started out of our car. In one fast move, he had

the jump on her. With his hand on his gun butt, pointing a finger at her, he bellowed: *"Stay in that there car lady, you and your gang had better not make any moves!"*

"Gang!" I questioned, "What gang? I have ten kids!"

"Shut-up!" he stammered, *"I have a mind to run yawl in!"*

I asked him if *"yawl"* referred to me, or my whole gang.

"Shut-up!" he repeated—even when I wasn't talking.

I advised him to calm himself, and either write me a ticket, or throw me in the *"hoosegow"*, but please take his finger out of my face. He accused me of being scatter-brained, while repeatedly referring to my car as a *"wreck"*…now that hurt!

He may have been correct about the mindlessness, after all, I was traveling 1300 miles with ten bickering kids, a loaded trailer, and a wife who reads road maps upside down, but I resented the part about my car, as any man would.

I asked for his name, and he stuck his name tag into my face, while yelling his badge number at me. I asked to borrow his pen and he lost control again. What a nervous cop I thought.

With trembling hands, he wrote me a "warning" and told me if he saw me and my wreck anywhere in the Carolinas, he would shot me on sight. With that, he popped his sombrero off his ears, mounted his charger, and skidded-off into the sunset…spraying me and my gang with road gravel. I'll bet if we had Carnivorous CoCo with us, he wouldn't have spoken that way.

Yes we made it home safely, simply because I'm always in total control during any crises. (There goes Anne reading over my shoulder and laughing again. What's so funny!)

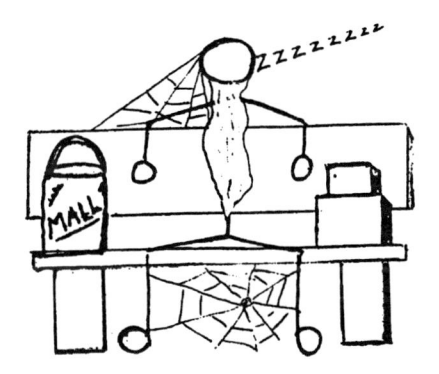

## Men on Mall Benches

There must be something wrong with me. I can't get excited about super jumbo malls expanded into small sized villages. Whatever happened to old-fashioned downtown: quaint shops, curb-front parking and hometown atmosphere that encouraged love thy neighbor, or even know thy neighbor?

I was recently dragged to a large mall by my shopaholic wife, who claims she can kick the addiction in just three months, yeah right…If I lock her in the basement between Thanksgiving Day and Easter Morning.

Instead of parking in front of the store of choice, we park in a colossal parking lot—sometimes used for emergency landings of 747s. The sign read **"YELLOW SECTION"**, which is suppose to help me find my car. It doesn't work. We boarded a shuttle bus for the last half mile trip to the main entrance.

Once inside, my shopping excitement heightened to a mild itch. There was a large registry indexing 237 stores, from a red arrow that said: **YOU ARE HERE!**" I was relieved to know someone knew where I was.

We took two escalators, one elevator, one potty stop and 10 minutes to rest my legs, lungs and limited patience, while Anne stood doing leg stretches to stay limber for the marathon. I noticed the usual assortment of benched husbands with cobwebs forming on white beards. I mustered the strength to go on— similar to an Indiana Jones, with my wife cracking the whip.

Finally reaching our destination, I was facing a young, glassy-eyed sales clerk in a semi-coma. I said good morning, and he answered: *"It is?"* I asked him a question about a product, and he said he didn't know what I was talking about. Why not, I asked. He said he was on loan from another department, proudly exclaiming he was in *"Panty Hose."* I asked selling or wearing? He said. "Both!"

*"Get me the manager!"*

The manager was younger than my newest suit. I asked if he had a particular item, and he said no. I asked if he even knew what it was, he said no. I asked rhetorically, what ever happened to the storekeeper who knew his stock and trade. This drop-out from Day School says: *"I don't know, I just started last month!"*

*"That's it!"* I shouted, *"let me out of here!"*

By now I'm ranting about how stupid it was to shop at a mall that had its own zip code and hired people with IQs lower than room temperature. When I looked around, I was standing red-faced in a gawking crowd of a few hundred customers. My wife, resembling an addict with the keys to a drug cabinet, had left to prowl the shops...all 237 of them.

I found a bench and sat next to someone with moss growing around his feet. I dozed off, dreaming I was browsing old-fashioned shops, overlooking a beautiful waterfront, with hometown charm—when I was blasted from my snooze by a PA system that could be heard in a two-mile radius. Some guy from Lost & Found was threatening a mother for the third and last time to, *"…come and pick-up your CRACKLE, CRACKLE, SNAP…kid!"*

My fellow bench-warmers never stirred. I realized why they were petrified, they had been waiting for the parking lot to clear so they could find their cars. I didn't have that problem; my car was in the **"BLUE SECTION,"** or was it **"GREEN"** ? Give me a break, I'm still trying to find Waldo and his five purple peacocks wearing pink pantaloons.

If malls start posting City Limits signs, I will not be visiting without my "Goofy" lunch box, bus transfers, and a Saint Bernard. It's upsetting to sit in Lost & Found for seven hours before my wife even knows she's misplaced me.

## "Picky, Picky, Picky"

My wife Anne is easy to please. She settles for the simplest gift and never overindulges luxuries. On occasion she has passed-up the Kapok Tree and Empress Lily restaurants, for the salad bar at Wendy's. But there is one privilege she demands total control over: choice of motel/hotel. I having driven till midnight with one eye open while she scrutinized the best of them. We have to find just *"the right one."*

In over 40 years of marriage and more than 100,000 road miles, I can say that more then 80 motor inns and hotels we have stayed in were the best by Anne's standards. Her checklist demands: Not too dirty. Not too dark. Not out-of-the way. Not mid-town. Not too cheap. Not too expensive. She has said: *"What can they offer for $39—one towel each?"* And when the price is over $60, her complaint is: *"They had better have 6 soft towels, and a continental breakfast with more than donut holes!"*

Inspections start in the parking lot. I have to cruise up and down the area, while she checks out the parked cars. Flashy cars and lack of out-of-town license plates assure her; *"This is a bordello, and we will be bothered all night with 'clients'"* Our two sons—both police detectives, would be proud of Ma.

She has hauled us from many motels after finding a broken "sanitary seal" on the toilet. Stale tobacco odor in a supposed "non-smoker" tells her the maid was holding afternoon gambling parties…and who knows what else! Economy priced, and top names have succumb to Anne's White Glove test.

Our children are trained in the art of self-defense used against the Inns of America, regardless of marquee name. It is true, daughters do inherit their mother's phobias, and peccadilloes. My daughters have been known to send their husbands packing before unpacking—over a dead bug. One even borrowed a vacuum cleaner from the bewildered late night desk clerk.

A death in the family necessitated a trip to New Jersey. My oldest daughter Theresa and her husband, came along. A busy season and late hour limited our choice of "just the right" room.

We settled for a room not to Anne's liking. It was clean, brand-named and reasonably priced. The flaw being it towered four stories above the ground.

Anne was convinced some drunk would set fire to the first three floors while we slept, refusing first to get on the elevator, and then off. While we pulled and pushed her into the second most fearful thing in her life, the first being open back stairs, She kept muttering *"Didn't you see the 'Towering Inferno?'"*

Settled into our P.J.'s Theresa pulled her trusted can of Lysol from her bag and began "disinfecting" the shower, toilet, rugs, air conditioning unit. Then the beds. Like her mother, she whipped the spread down and eye-balled the sheets. She screamed *"Ahhh!"* to which mother, who instinctively jumped on the other bed responded; *"What is it?…is it alive?"*, *"Get off that bedspread…"* Theresa turned again to her mother. *"Don't put your body on the top bedspread! You don't know who was lying there!."* Mother was bouncing around the room with every hysterical demand.

Theresa just knew, beyond doubt, that housekeeping was renting rooms to street people, and who knew what we may catch.

Her husband refused to argue with the desk clerk over the stained sheet when the clerk told him to sleep on it, it won't bite you. That sent Anne and Theresa scrambling for the phone. Theresa won the contest and said: *"Listen to me you little twerp, I want new sheets or a new room. If not, I call the Better Business Bureau!"* "Please lady..." pleaded the clerk, *"it's after midnight, go to sleep. I promise the stain won't hurt you!"*

Theresa tried sending her husband down to the front desk to demand clean ones. He refused on grounds of insanity—hers! I remained semi-conscious in a chair, since I had driven 600 miles and had more than one spot before my eyes.

In minutes, Theresa and her ma were at the reception desk, piling the sheets under the nose of a guest begging for a room. Theresa turned to the man and said; *"A stain! Look at that, for $42, I get a stain! What kind of a room is that!"* The customer, tired and roomless said; *"I'll take it!...I'll take it!"*

All this time, mother is arguing with an assistant about not have enough fire extinguishes in the rooms. One per room wasn't enough. She was demanding a unit next to each bed.

The security guard whisked us bag and baggage to another room. Theresa was warning him that the sheets had better be clean, while mother was in his other ear pleading with him; *"Don't you have something closer to the ground!"*

It was a sleepless night for three of us. Theresa popped-up looking for bugs. Mother sniffed for smoke. And her husband snored. "What's that?"..."Sniff, sniff"..."Zzzzzzzzzz"...

## "Restaurants Everywhere…But No Place to Eat"

My wife claims I'm as bad or worse at choosing restaurants, as she is at picking motels. There is no way that is possible.

*"How would you like to go to "Wendy's for a salad bar dinner?"* I asked Anne, *"Great!"* she said.

Since she had to feed the six piranha first, it was 6:30 when we reached the counter. As we approached—famished, we heard the counter girl yell at her manager; *"I want to go home…now!"* Without the pleasantries afforded paying customers she barked at us: *"Your order?!"* without a *"howdy"*, or even *"please"*. Just an icy stare and an angry look. All I said to her was: *"Why are you mad at me, I didn't make your schedule!"* Right away Anne gives me the elbow in my rib and says; *"Don't start!"*

The girl lacked the required head covering or at least proper tie-backs for her untamed mop of hair. Her frizzed-out orange colored Punk Rocker Do was all over the place, and I was sure it would be in my food. Aside from her attitude and appearance, she needed the help of a Dermatologist, fast—*"like before I ate my meal…man!"*

85

Anne, with great anticipation of a salad bar invasion, said: *"I'll take a..."* when I gave her a "gentle" shove toward the door, telling the orange colored peacock with the "tude" that we were outta here: *"...forget it, I've lost my appetite!"*

Stumbling out the door, Anne asked: *"What happened?"*

*"Never mind..."* I said, *"I want the mood right. If I want aggravation from snotty teenagers I'd stay at home. Where do you want to go next?"*

*"Next?"* Anne said, *"Have we been somewhere yet?"*

I asked her to pick a restaurant, any restaurant. She said: *"Anywhere, I'm hungry!"* We sounded like the Marty movie: *"I don't know, Marty, where do you want to go?"*

*"I don't know, where do you want to go!"*

We *almost* ate at five restaurants in two hours. The choices were running out—and so was the time. I was trying to avoid noise, crowds, overpricing and the stench of stale smoke and booze. There is a difference between a restaurant with a lounge, and a beer joint with sandwiches, deviled eggs and pigs feet.

Anne was as upset with my hairsplitting, as I would get with her choice of the right motel. Where I would be tired, she was hungry. Boy, was she hungry. I could hear her stomach growling.

The Brown Derby was crowded, as was the Western Sizzler.

*"How about the Pizza Hut?"* she asked, half pleading.

A waitress pointed us to a corner booth and ordered:

*"Sit!...I'll be right back!"* I felt like I was being paper trained. *"Where's her swastika and boots?"* I mussed. Anne not amused said: *"Don't start again, I'm starving!"*

I sat obediently at my pepperoni smeared table, and on soda soiled seat. All I said was, when do they clean-up here, at closing time?

And Anne said quiet. Who would hear me? The speaker over head was knocking the wax out of my ears with Hard Rock, while a Punk Rocker in the next booth pounded his table supposedly to the music. He was totally unaware that God had not blessed him with rhythm, being at least two beats off the mark.

Across the sauce splattered aisle, a six year old and his brother in dripping shorts, were spitting coke at each other through straws, each spray coming closer to my brand new pants.

*"What do you expect, It's family night!"* Anne said, as if that made the food stains, noise and headache O.K. *"Oh, is that what it is?"* I asked. *"I thought we were home!"*

I asked if she knew that when we came in, or was it a trace of sadistic cruelty.

*"Where are we going now?"* asked Anne, as we drove away.

*"How about the new Seafood Grille?"* I offered.

After giving the maitre d' a fictitious name, which I find easier than listening to them butcher Squitieri over the P.A., *Mr. and Mrs. Fish* waited in the lobby with 20 other growling stomachs. One half hour went by, and all I asked the alias Mrs. Fish was did she think it was worth waiting in line for $12.95 Rainbow Trout? Before I knew it, she handed the maitre d' the menu and was out the door. *"Something wrong Sir?"* he asked, *"Oh, no, Mrs. Fish gets like that when she's hungry!"*

About 9 p.m. when we settled on a restaurant. The atmosphere was void of smoke and noise. The food was good and plentiful, and well priced. The waitress didn't speak with a French accent, but was very pleasant. It turned-out *The Red Lobster* satisfied us, but I think by then, *Nathan's* would have sufficed.

Out in the parking lot I asked: *"How about some ice cream?"* *"Depends..."* Anne said, *"How many ice cream parlors are there in the county?"*

As I dragged her to the car, she said: *"Here we go again!"*

## An Offer You Can't Refuse

We have all had that unhappy experience of selling the family car. It is more traumatic to the man than the wife, since it's his long time faithful buddy, but to her—nothing more than an old piece of junk the Jones next door wouldn't drive.

The old wagon has been a loyal friend and servant. It has given 110,000 happy miles and has become a part of Dad's very being, but it has to go. Putting a *"For Sale"* sign on it equal to one third it's worth is degrading. He is convinced it's worth much more than $450, but no one else is.

At first, knowing it's full value, he will take it in to a used car lot as a trade-in. But *Honest John's Used Cars* won't have anything to do with it. He says *"It's junk"*…but if you trade on this year's *"Honey"*, sticker priced at only $18,000, he'll give you $200 on paper, and wholesale the "junk" for $300.

How about those $1.25 Want Ads. But lady, you ask, it says 1.25? *"Right, but anything more then "For Sale" is extra!"* So you spent $15 and wait for the crazies to start calling. The same people who come to your garage sales, trying to by collectable antiques for .25 cents, like you're an idiot.

*"What kind of shape is the car in?"* Think about that one. I'm selling a 12 year old car for $450…and it runs! The operative word here is *"used"*…a word they seem to ignore.

Well I'd say it is in mint condition, absolutely stunning. I'm thinking of putting it in the Auto Museum.

*"I don't want a car I have to fix!"* Another goody. Neither do I, you nitwit, that's why I'm selling it! If you want a *"Reconditioned Used Car"* with a 30 day warranty, go see Honest John and pay $1,800.

*"Do you guarantee it will run?"* I sure do. For $450 I guarantee it to the end of my driveway, then you're on your own. Give me a break. I put $2,432 into it to reach 110,000 miles, now it's your turn.

My daughter bought a car from a "friend"—using that term lightly. She did her a favor and only charged $500. Just three days later, a rod blew in the engine. The friend failed to warn my daughter about the "Heat tape" that is suppose to be turned-on every cold winter's night. It will cost her $500 for a used engine, plus labor. Here I am selling a whole car that runs for $50 less, ashtrays and all!

Which brings me to the last alternative: *"Friendly Freddy's Car Morgue"* out Booney Road on God's forgotten area. It is just past Dead Man's Curve, where they pick-up most of their inventory, better known as Smashed Metal Road Kills.

His reaction to your lowered asking price of $200 is an uncontrolled bare-belly laugh, which hangs over his grease stained jeans—jeans that have been standing-up on their own for a forth night. Sounding like Honest John, he sneers: *"We don't want that junk!"* When it's coming in it's worthless junk, when it's going out, it's priceless merchandise.

He appears uninterested and independent. He lays-out the ground rules: If you drive it in: $50. If you push it in, $25. If he has to come to your house to pick-up the remains—you pay the reaper. How sweet it is. They buy the thing for $25, strip it down to its bits and pieces: starter, battery, doors, fenders, door handles, mirrors, gas caps and ashtrays. Than this piece of worthless junk brings back $2,500. Your engine, if you should want to buy it back, will cost you $450.

It's a battle you can't win. They get you buying and selling. I'm tempted to drive Old Faithful into a field and shot a hole in its block head and let it rest in pieces. No money grubbing over its remains. But we are not allowed by law to let metal decay in a field, nor can we bury O' Grandpa on the hill, or Rover near the creek.

So folks, step right up. Can I interest you in a good used starter? How about a windshield…cheap! Maybe a rear seat?…a front door?…rear bumper?…

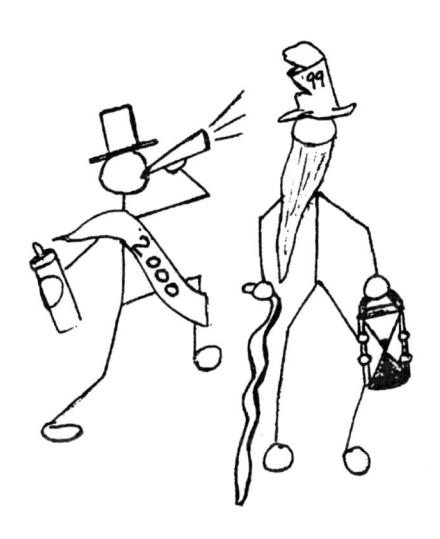

## Someday Was Yesterday

Someday has arrived. Life had passed like a flash of light, leaving Mama and Papa bird alone. When the dust settled all ten chicks had left the nest, and we were a couple again. But it wasn't the same. It seemed we were surrounded with kids from the moment the priest pronounced us husband and wife and longed for the peace and quiet we mistakenly thought we wanted. We soon realized we don't miss what we never had, but do miss what we once had and lost. The nest is painfully deserted, and the silence deafening.

Along with those lonely quite days, you'll find two other sorrowful parts of life: old age, and its synonym, ailments. It is inevitable since the body breaks down with age and use—or misuse. We all have the normal aches, pains and complaints, but on occasion, the illness can be a serious one. In my case, at the age of 55 I came down with an incurable autoimmune disease: Polymyositis. My immune system had turned-around and was destroying my muscle. The *Watch-Dog* was confusing the good guys with the bad guys. Dozens of tests and doctors told me it was incurable, and took $52,000 to prove it.

I prefix that to tell you this: your true sense of humor should not and will not leave you in the midst of trouble, sorrow or illness. In fact, it will sustain you. The Book of Proverbs tells us: *"A merry heart doeth good like a medicine, but a broken spirit drieth the bones."*

I spent four of the five years of illness upstairs in my three room prison, unable to make stairs, shower alone, or dress myself, I managed to retain my sanity through my sense of humor. By looking for the humor in difficulties, even tragedy, helped myself, and my family get through some horrendous times, which included the death of our twenty four year old son.

You had better have a sense of what's funny, and a deep abiding Faith and Trust in God. Nothing else can get you through, when all the world is crushing down on you. Your foundation had better be The Rock, and His Supporting Arms.

Before I found my cure through a skilled French Canadian Naturopath using Homeopathy, the five years of imprisonment called for some strong ability to *"laugh it off!"* and we did.

*Case in point:*

Due to my loss of muscle, I fell down a lot. Falling wasn't so bad, getting up was the problem. It seemed every time I went down I was alone. However, in almost every instance, my faithful companion "Grace" was there. She is my omnipresent cat. She never left my side and made those months of confinement bearable. One of those unplanned trips happened on a Friday evening, which is ladies night out. It is something my wife, sister and daughters do each week. They call it "wings" I'm not sure if it is something they eat, or the fact they were flying the coup—as in coup d'e 'tat.

They had brought my Friday night dinner of fresh fish and fries—hot juicy and delicious. My cat Grace, thought as much, followed it into the living room. My family thought I would be alright alone downstairs for a while. They were not all right.

I sat on my built-up cushioned chair,(which had become standard equipment since I could not get up alone) eating my dinner on a wood serving table before me. As I sat in the darkened living room watching TV, Grace sat on her perch, a wooden radiator cover just to my left shoulder. She was licking her chops, and whining; *"Where's mine?"*

I told her to come down and take a piece of my fish. I didn't eat her food, but was willing to share mine. Being a cat, she wouldn't move. You cat owners know how independent and stubborn they can be.

She said, in so many unspoken words, I'm not moving, you bring the fish to me! Being a good pet owner, and obligated to the feline for years of companionship and unconditional love, I reluctantly gave in.

While threatening to send her to the "road kill" canning factory, I got up to serve the spoiled prissy. With one eye on the TV program, and the other eye on Grace, I should have had a third eye to watch where I was going. My feet got tangled-up in the table legs. Me, the table and the fish dinner went down. Grace the fink, ran upstairs.

There I laid, spread out across the fish and fries, with the table on my back, and a rug burn on my forehead where the third eye should have been. I would have continued my Pete Rose slide, but the sofa stopped me, adding a bump to the rug burn.

Having no arm or leg muscles to lift myself, or eyeglasses to see with, there was no way I was getting up from the rug. I had to move along the sofa, sitting on my tush. Making it into the office—a good twenty minute trip on a quiet night, I found both phones up out of reach. I used a yard stick to knock the wireless phone from its cradle, a brilliant move, since it had its dial attached, and the kitchen wall phone was five feet above me. I was feeling clever, when the phone fell behind a fully loaded file cabinet.

With the muscle of a bantam weight pygmy, I tried wrestling the steel cabinet. It was Unmovable. I returned to the yardstick, using it to fish the phone out, taking longer than the trip.

Thankfully, one of my daughters had not gone "winging" and came flying over with her two sons. They watched in amazement, while their mom lifted Pop Pop off the floor. An embarrassing position. Meantime, Grace, the one responsible for all this, ate my dinner. She left the bun, fries, and a bit of fish—on the bump, over the rug burn where the third eye should have been.

*******

The highlight of my days were meals. It broke-up the monotony of being alone. This major event was entertaining and fattening. But eating brought another problem: my ability to choke on everything I ate. The muscle disease had effected my esophagus causing the inability to swallow. If it was not liquefied to almost baby food texture, I'd choke.

I could not swallow solid pieces of meat. It had to be diced. All I ate, I "regurgitated" to keep from choking to death. Anything stringy was out: string beans, full length spaghetti, or artichoke—its name alone was forbidding.

Regurgitating sounded awful, but kept me alive—off color, but still breathing. Among family, not a problem. Dinner guests? Another story.

It takes a while to get our division of troops settled into the mess tent, after which food is passed left and right, while going right and left. Holidays, such as Thanksgiving, Christmas, New Year, and Easter, will find 18 to 20 men, woman and children around two tables in adjoining kitchen and dinning rooms. Flabbergasted dinner guests just sit staring. The commotion, which is nothing less than organized mayhem, is obviously mesmerizing. They have trouble keeping up with talk and motion.

While everyone was busy getting their spoils of battle, I had to concentrate on staying alive. Each time I would make the regurgitating sound, the unaware dinner quests would look around the room trying to locate that infernal noise.

A family member, between morsels, would brush it off as: *"That's just Dad choking!"* and go on eating. The dumbfounded guests, staring at me with fork half way to their mouths, were most likely thinking *"My God, will he croak before desert?"*

Another forbidden fruit was the orange. Had Eve fed one to Adam-instead of the supposed apple, life on earth as we know it, might have ended on the Sixth Day. If not, it would have been the pizza cheese.

One morning, while my daughter Arlene the "RX Tech" was getting ready for work—still living home at that time, I got a piece of stringy orange stuck in my throat. Over the noise of a radio in her ear, and a hair dryer stuck in her other ear, I managed to get her attention before the last pictures of my life passed before my popping eyes. By the time she came into my room, the chorus of "nearer my God to thee" was over, and my heliotrope rash had turned a pretty shade of blue.

My eyes bugging-out of my head wasn't enough of a clue to my impending demise. I was doing pantomime, gesturing toward the orange, then my mouth, while she kept asking; *"What?...What?"*

Finally, after my imitation of a hanging, she got the message. *"You're choking!"* Right! Now ain't she the smart one ? Makes me proud to think she got it on the fourth try. Using a generic version of the Heimlich Maneuver, she swatted my mid-back with the force of a sledgehammer, throwing the loosened obstruction across the room. All this while yelling at me as though I were a bad boy! *"No more oranges! I can't take these scares before work!"*

After my second full breath, I apologized to her, and told her I'd arrange my next choking on her day off.

You can imagine how many tests and exams I was given in the four years of illness, especially since they did not know what caused the disease, or how to cure it. I was used as—excuse the ethnic slur, a guinea pig. A large percentage of the tests were to monitor damage being done by the immunosuppressant drug I was taking. The steroid, Prednisone, was the only answer they had to quite the disease. It should only be taken at the extreme for 3 months, I was on it for four years. The drug can do its own damage, without a hint of a cure. A sense of humor had to stay the frustration.

The oath taken at Med School says: *"Pri-mum non nucere"* which translates don't hurt the patient while trying to help him. Ya right! The test made me sicker than the disease. Over the first three years I was drugged, poked, pinched, gagged, fingered, biopsied, X-rayed, cat scanned, lung scoped, spine tapped, stood on my head, force-fed barium, irrigated by rubber hose (both ends) illuminated and constipated. The problem was not just finding how much damage the drugs were doing, but trying to make up their minds if the disease came from cancer or caused cancer. Thus $52,000 in mostly useless and damaging testing.

Eventually the frustration and anger was getting to me. I thought I had better handle it with humor. After all, I'm the pokee, and I'm the one paying for their fun.

When a specialist tried switching me to a new drug, I refused. He tried convincing me by saying the drug only caused one fatality: a Roman Catholic nun. Great. She had the Pope and the whole Catholic Church on her side, and it still killed her. Me being a proselyte, what chance did I have. He didn't think that was funny, neither did I. I refused the drug.

When ever I'm told about a drug having bad side effects or reactions, I question the odds. When I'm told there is only a one percent chance I'd have problems, I pass. My luck stinks.

As for testing, I was nuked so many times, my wife uses me for a reading lamp. Body scans, head scans, lung scopes, X-rays, you name it, I've had it. Boy had I had it.

While being prepared for the "tunnel" and more pictures, a nurse was trying unsuccessfully to get a catheter into the back of my right hand. It wasn't going any better then the left hand. I was looking like a bloody piece of Swiss cheese, when I asked for a doctor. I got one with an attitude. He asked me what was my problem I said I didn't have one, his nurse did. I asked him if he ever had these tests, and like all the M.D.s before him, he said no. I told him it was no picnic, so just get me poked and nuked and get it over with.

When she finally got the radioactive fluids flowing, I asked her what was this stuff pouring out of my ears. She went ballistic. She was running around the table, and bunking into herself, yelling: *"Where?...What?"* I told her to relax, I'm only joking. She said it wasn't funny. I said neither was the fact that she didn't know where it should go in or come out!

The next step was lung test number four. I was again on my back. I had looked at more ceilings than a well used hooker. Again, the nurse was having trouble getting a gas mask to stay on my mouth. They were attempting to fill my lungs with more radioactive gas. She was frustrated with the thing because it kept popping apart. She called her supervisor for advice. The one getting the big bucks said: *"Use more tuck tape!"* I kid you not folks! You can't create anything this silly.

The female Laurel and Hardy weren't done yet. They rolled in a table containing storage tanks of gas and oxygen. When one of them threw a switch fireworks started popping from the table. With rockets red glare and sparks bursting in air, the nurses ran for the hallway. I could see them not thinking it worth $18.00 per hour to die in the line of fire, but my wife ran with them, leaving me strapped to the table. What happened to "'till death do we part!"? She was ahead, of the oath...and the nurses.

When it appeared it wasn't going to blow and take me with it, they returned to my side and continued the job of gassing me with the hose and tuck tape. When I told her it wasn't nice to run away and leave me there, she stuck the mask on my face and said: *"Breathe...deep, deep breaths!"*

It was an unpleasant five years. But thank God, I found a doctor in Canada whom I was led to by circumstances the Lord had provided. I was cured of an incurable disease and, as the doctor predicted, back to work in exactly one year. But folks, that's another book you'll just have to read.

## ...And Then There Were None

As I said in the beginning, life has had many changes for Anne and myself. From childhood lovers, to mother and father of ten children. Anne has been through much with me. But through it all she has kept her promise to stay by me through riches and poverty, sickness and health, and almost till death did we part. When she is told there would be bad times as well as good, she asked: *"When do the good times start?"*

We are older, alone and less durable. But God has a way of comforting His own, even when what we wished for wasn't what we thought we wanted: Peace and quite. He came up with a great idea called Grandchildren. Grandkids to me are like the Three Stooges. They are funny, but I can only take in small doses. Although Anne tells me we only have three or four visiting at one time, I know that isn't true. At any given moment, there are at least a dozen. I know, I saw them moving in a deafening flash.

Even as I speak, here come two of God's Blessings up the driveway. I call them *"Instigate"* and *"Agitate"*. Grandma is elevating her knickknacks out of reach, something she never had to do with her own kids, and I'm "hiding" my Devil Dogs in a conspicuous place…

As life comes full circle…